JUDICIAL CONTROLS AND THE CIVIL LITIGATIVE PROCESS:  DISCOVERY

Paul R. Connolly
Edith A. Holleman
Michael J. Kuhlman

Federal Judicial Center
June, 1978

# CONTENTS

Examining the evolution of the Federal Rules of Civil Procedure reveals a gradual relaxation of rule control over the discovery process at the very time that the scope of discovery was expanding.  The changing rule structure placed increasing dependence upon attorney initiative to police the scope and pace of discovery.  As prescriptive rules disappeared, rule 83 loomed ever larger as the primary source of judicial authority to manage the flow of litigation, including discovery.  Rule 37 provided for judicial leverage in the management of discovery timing, but its exercise depends upon attorneys.

The Compelling Process.  Data disclose that most discovery responses are not filed within the thirty-day period provided by the federal rules.  Requesting parties rarely ask for compelling orders, and when they do seek court assistance, they do not do so promptly.  Rulings on motions for compelling orders overwhelmingly favor the moving party.

The Sanction Process.  Sanction motions are rarely filed, despite the fact that most judicial rulings on sanction motions result in grantings.

Conclusion.  Reliance on court control of discovery through attorney initiative under rule 37 is ineffective in securing timeliness.

Recorded Discovery.  Court records provide a satisfactory measure of total discovery activity, even though unrecorded discovery events account for approximately one-quarter of discovery exchanges between parties.

Extent of Discovery Use.  More than half of the terminated cases under study had no recorded discovery requests.  Less than 5 percent of the 3,114 cases had more than ten requests.
Depositions are the most frequently used discovery device, followed by interrogatories and document requests.  All other types collectively account for only 7 percent of discovery requests.
Discovery-related motions punctuate the discovery period. Cases with low-volume discovery (one or two requests) will have about one motion per seven cases.  Very high-volume cases (more than thirty requests) will have about nine motions per case.

Discovery Abuse. The data do not speak directly to questions of discovery abuse, but the modest number of discovery events suggests that abuse, to the extent it exists, will be found in the quality of discovery activity rather than in the quantity of discovery requests.

Effective discovery timing controls require informed estimates of discovery activity. Case characteristics evident in the pleadings provide early signals of the probable discovery activity in a case.

Selecting a Management Track. Certain types of litigation involve so little discovery and are so frequently disposed of by motion that they should be managed on a motion control rather than a discovery control track.

Factors Affecting the Amount of Discovery. The subject matter of a case, the number of parties, the presence of counterclaims or cross claims, and, to a lesser extent, the amount in controversy, are reliable predictors of the amount of discovery that will be sought.

Effects of Judge Control on Overall Discovery Times. Strong discovery controls require (1) consistency in application, (2) early announcement, (3) relatively short periods, and (4) firm adherence to cutoff dates.
Cases before judges who use strong controls have discovery periods five to eight months shorter than cases not subject to such controls. The discovery period is shortened in cases with low, moderate, and high volumes of discovery.

Effects of Combined Judge and Court Control on Overall Discovery Times. A strong-control court environment increases the time saved in the discovery period for all judges--both those who use strong controls and those who use limited or no controls.

Control and Patterns of Requesting Discovery. The use of strong discovery timing controls does not reduce the amount of discovery requested by the parties. Cases subject to strong controls exhibit the same patterns of discovery requests as cases subject to limited or no controls.

Control and Response Time. Responses to discovery requests are prompter in cases subject to strong controls for all types of discovery requests, though the amount saved varies by type. Imposition of controls does not result in greater use of compelling motions.

Initiation Time. Part of the savings in overall discovery time resulting from controls is realized by shorter times between discovery requests. Gaps of inactivity between discovery initiatives are substantially shortened.

Effects of Control on Stages of the Litigative Process. Cases subject to strong controls over discovery time exhibit shorter times for the pleadings, discovery, and pretrial stages. Trial time shows very little effect from discovery controls. Total disposition time is shortened for cases subject to strong controls, whether the cases terminate by trial or by settlement.

Contributions of Non-Discovery Time to Total Disposition Time. Shortened time in non-discovery stages among cases subject to discovery timing controls suggests that judges and courts using strong discovery controls use them in a comprehensive case management system that affects the entire litigative process.

Pleadings and Discovery. Imposition of discovery timing controls does not cause attorneys to initiate discovery before answers are filed. Therefore, the benefits observed in cases subject to control can be achieved by imposition of controls after joinder of issue.

Enlargements of the Discovery Control Period. Enlargement motions and the consequent burden on judges and attorneys are reduced when cutoff dates are applied on a case-by-case basis. A uniform discovery control period applied to all cases appears unrealistic. Case-by-case application should require, as a condition of enlargement, a showing of diligent discovery during the allotted period and specific needs justifying more time.

Effect of Discovery Timing Control on Scheduling the Final Pretrial Conference. Simultaneous establishment of a cutoff date and a date for the final pretrial conference provides an effective termination of the discovery period and eliminates periods of inactivity between completion of discovery and the final pretrial conference.

Limited Judicial Resources and the Use of Discovery Timing Controls. Savings in total disposition time will depend upon a credible trial date, a condition that may not always be possible. Shortened discovery time periods, however, can be achieved even if trial days are not available. Early completion of discovery has benefits beyond its contribution to shortened disposition time.

A discovery timing control model that incorporates the relationships observed in the data from the study courts is recommended. A simple formula expresses the amount of discovery activity likely to occur when major predictive characteristics are present. Predicted activity is translated into recommended allotment of discovery time.

LIST OF TABLES

## LIST OF FIGURES

# FOREWORD

This report should be viewed as a beginning. It explores from one perspective the operation of the federal rules governing discovery as revealed in more than 7,000 docketed requests appearing in more than 3,000 terminated cases in six United States district courts. (A survey of practitioners in the six districts suggests that the docketed requests cover the great bulk of discovery activity.) The report is a continuation of the Center's District Court Studies Project, the first report of which (Case Management and Court Management in United States District Courts) appeared several months ago.

The instant report does not study "discovery abuse" as such, or even attempt a rigorous definition. Its data, however, are relevant to widespread concerns that the discovery process consumes too much time, too much energy, and too much money. As the report itself indicates:

> It is possible for a single discovery request to be abusive, as it is possible for sixty-two requests to be appropriate, relevant, and facilitative in the just disposition of a particular case. The data do suggest, however, that discovery abuse, to the extent it exists, does not permeate the vast majority of federal filings. In half the filings, there is no discovery--abusive or otherwise. In the remaining half of the filings, abuse--to the extent it exists--must be found in the quality of the discovery requests, not in the quantity, since fewer than 5 percent of the filings involved more than ten requests.

Furthermore, despite the common view that federal judges will not impose sanctions under rule 37, the data show that sanctions, although rarely sought, are indeed frequently granted. Fewer than 1 percent of the requests led to motions for sanctions, but the motions were granted in about three-fourths of those that led to rulings. If analysis of data from other courts, yielding larger numbers of motions, shows the same trend, there may be cause to wonder whether the pessimism about the effectiveness of rule 37 is a self-fulfilling prophecy.

One of the most cogent findings in this report is that the imposition of what the report defines as "strong judicial controls" will shorten the time consumed by discovery without impairing discovery rights. Shortened discovery time is in turn associated with shortened case disposition time. Although this report is a beginning, more will be learned from a series of Center projects already under way, designed to expand our knowledge of various aspects of civil litigation. Among these inquiries are two sets of case studies, one exploring the details of the high-volume discovery cases revealed in this report, another probing cases identified by practitioners as exhibiting discovery problems. This Center research will further refine and augment our knowledge of what indeed is happening in the federal courts, what is causing it, and, where appropriate, what might be done about it.

A. Leo Levin
Director

## ACKNOWLEDGMENTS

This report has involved a collective effort by members of the Federal Judicial Center's family and friends. Their hard work and devotion, as much as a compelling need to study the judicial management of discovery, made the report a reality.

We could not hope to fully acknowledge in this brief space the contributions of each participant. Every description here represents many hours of work, and carries with it our deep appreciation of a job well and amiably done.

We begin by thanking Judge Walter E. Hoffman and Professor A. Leo Levin, the two Center directors under whose auspices this report was begun and completed. Both Judge Hoffman and Professor Levin have lent their considerable talents to fostering an understanding of case and court management, particularly the judicial management of discovery.

Working on a statistical report of this magnitude required asking myriad questions--questions that might have gone unanswered but for the wisdom and experience of Joseph L. Ebersole, deputy director of the Center, and William B. Eldridge, director of the Center's Research Division. Mr. Ebersole conceived and guided the District Court Studies Project from its infancy. Mr. Eldridge had the skill and patience to teach us the art and science of research; his contributions lent clarity and style to our final draft. Both men provided constructive criticism at every stage.

The idea of a statistical description of the civil litigative process originated with Steven Flanders, director of the District Court Studies Project, and John Lederer, then a law clerk to Judge Hoffman and now in private practice. Steve saw the need to collect "hard" data on court performance; John helped develop the methodology used to collect and process the data, and took valuable time from his practice to help surmount unforeseen roadblocks.

Much of the statistical analysis was undertaken by three very talented statisticians--Gary Oleson, under contract to the Center, and Michael R. Leavitt and Pat Lombard of the Center's research staff. Gary helped design the data collection instrument and the calculations used to process the data. Mike helped overcome hurdles in the methodology and the analysis. Pat worked with us for more than a year--running calculations, performing statistical analyses, commenting on methodology, reviewing drafts, and verifying data. Her professional skill was surpassed only by her industry and her cheerfulness.

xiii

Anne Myerson Ayers, senior editor at the Center, gave unstintingly of her time and skills to produce the final report. Research is only as good as the vehicle that communicates it; Anne sought to ensure that the report communicated its findings clearly. We are deeply appreciative of her assistance. Helping Anne was a dedicated, patient, and efficient production team: Carolyn H. McGinnis, who produced the camera-ready copy; Myrna L. Brantley, who typed our raw manuscript; and Patricia A. Hughes, who typed early drafts and many figures and tables.

Others who contributed significantly to this study also deserve our thanks. Marlene Maddelone, Alan Shermer, and Henry Garden worked long hours collecting the data. Larry Goldberg and Roxanne Scott provided research assistance. Staff in the clerk's offices of the six courts we visited cooperated fully with us, despite our disruptions of their routines. W.R. King and George S. Bridges of the Justice Department's Office for Improvements in the Administration of Justice reviewed our drafts and made several helpful suggestions.

We are greatly indebted to certain members of the federal judiciary. Judge Hubert L. Will of the Northern District of Illinois and Judge Alexander Harvey II of the District of Maryland took considerable time from their busy schedules to review our manuscript. Their recommendations led to many changes in the analysis. Finally, lawyers might not enter the field of judicial administration research unless they were inspired by the example of members of the judiciary. Our inspiration came from three judges for whom one or another of us has clerked: Judge David W. Dyer of the Fifth Circuit Court of Appeals, Judge Oren R. Lewis of the Eastern District of Virginia, and Judge James Lawrence King of the Southern District of Florida. By their actions, each of them gave meaning to the mandate of rule 1 of the Federal Rules of Civil Procedure: "to secure the just, speedy, and inexpensive determination of every action." In the art of judging, each of these men is a consummate craftsman. Our apprenticeship with them yielded immense rewards.

Of course, none of the individuals named above are responsible for any errors in the data or in interpretation, for which we take full responsibility.

Paul R. Connolly
Edith A. Holleman
Michael J. Kuhlman

# INTRODUCTION

> To no man will we deny justice,
> to no man will we delay justice.
> Magna Carta, 1215

After quoting King John's promise of justice without delay, Judge Irving R. Kaufman (then a district judge, now Chief Judge of the Second Circuit), stated that "almost 750 years later, that great and simple pledge has not yet been completely fulfilled."[1] Reiterating Chief Justice Earl Warren's concern with the "interminable and unjustifiable delays in our courts," Judge Kaufman noted that the late Chief Justice had appealed to judges "to bring the full prestige of your judicial office to bear at every stage of litigation to ensure promptness and efficiency."[2]

Continuing this quest for efficient judicial administration, the present Chief Justice, Warren E. Burger, in presenting the keynote address at the 1976 National Conference on the Causes of Popular Dissatisfaction with the Administration of Justice, urged that steps be taken to "'deliver' justice at the lowest possible cost in the shortest feasible time."[3]

A significant consequence of the 1976 conference was the report of the Pound Conference Follow-Up Task Force.[4] The task force cited criticism of the operation of the rules of discovery[5] and observed that empirical data might help produce remedies for the perceived problems in discovery.[6]

The Federal Judicial Center's District Court Studies Project was

---

1. Kaufman, _The Philosophy of Effective Judicial Supervision Over Litigation_, 29 F.R.D. 207, 215 (1961)

2. _Id._ at 207.

3. Burger, _Agenda for 2000 A.D.--A Need for Systematic Anticipation_, 70 F.R.D. 83, 89 (1976).

4. 74 F.R.D. 159 (1976).

5. _Id._ at 191.

6. _Id._ at 192. The 1965 report to the Advisory Committee on Rules of Civil Procedure described the first major empirical study of the operation of the federal discovery process. The study, Field Survey of Federal Pretrial Discovery, was conducted under the supervision of Professor Maurice Rosenberg, by the Columbia University School of Law's Project for Effective Justice. A subsequent report reanalyzed the Columbia survey data. W. Glaser, Pretrial Discovery and the Adversary System (1968) [hereinafter cited as Glaser report]. It should be noted that comparisons between the statistics in this study and those in the Glaser report are risky because of substantial methodological differences.

launched to study how judicial administration could eliminate unnecessary delays in federal litigation and increase the productivity of the federal trial courts. The project's findings are detailed in a series of three reports. In addition to this report, the District Court Study Series includes a summary document[7] and a forthcoming report on motions. This discovery report is an empirical study of the measures judges use to manage the civil discovery process.

The data base for the project, including this report, consists of all information recorded for about 500 terminated cases in each of six courts chosen for study. This total case population of more than 3,000 cases provided the statistical data to support the observations and conclusions offered in the discovery report.[8]

There was some concern that the data might not represent all discovery activity between the parties. A telephone survey of randomly selected attorneys in the six courts studied indicated, however, that about three-quarters of all discovery requests and responses are filed with the court.[9] This leads us to believe that the data collected are a reliable reflection of discovery activity.

The federal rules expressly mandate the "just, _speedy_, and inexpensive determination of every action."[10] The basis for this policy was articulated by Judge Walter E. Hoffman of the Eastern District of Virginia, a former director of the Federal Judicial Center. He specified two compelling reasons for judges to "take special responsibility to assure that cases are handled speedily. First, there is a public demand for all matters--business, personal, and legal--to be handled promptly."[11] Second,

---

7. S. Flanders, Case Management and Court Management in United States District Courts (Federal Judicial Center 1977) [hereinafter cited as Case Management report].

8. See appendix A for a description of how the data for this study were collected and a summary of the methodology used in the entire District Court Studies Project.

9. See appendix C.

10. Fed. R. Civ. P. 1 (emphasis added).

11. Hoffman, _Foreword_ to Case Management report, _supra_ note 7, at vii. _See_ B. Curran, The Legal Needs of the Public, table 6.2, at 229 (American Bar Foundation 1977) [hereinafter cited as Curran]. _See also_ National Center for State Courts, The Public Image of Courts: Highlights of a National Survey of the General Public, Judges, Lawyers and Community Leaders, tables II.5 & II.6, at 19-20 (1978) [hereinafter cited as The Public Image]. (In this survey of the public's views about court system performance, 11 percent of those surveyed indicated that their principal reason for unfavorable reactions to their civil court experience was that the "[c]ourt took too long [and was] too slow." Table II.5, at 19. Of those who had a favorable reaction, only 1 percent stated that the principal reason was "[q]uick, prompt action." Table II.6, at 20.)

speedy civil adjudications help the courts meet the two other central goals of the federal rules:  to determine every action both justly and inexpensively.[12]

Statistical reports prepared by the Administrative Office of the United States Courts show wide differences between district courts in disposition times of civil cases.[13]  The extent of this disparity strongly suggests that the objectives of rule 1 are not being uniformly attained throughout the federal system.  This problem is of concern not only to the judiciary, but also to the general public.[14]

The central finding of the summary report in the project series is that the judiciary's use of effective case and court management techniques can help speed the termination of civil actions without impairing the quality of justice.[15]  One prominent technique is the use of "automatic" procedures to assure that "discovery begins quickly and is completed within a reasonable time."[16]  This study has found that the regular use of discovery time controls can shorten discovery time and can consequently reduce overall disposition time of civil cases.

---

12.  Judge Hoffman suggested that the deterioration of evidence, and other "slipups" caused by delay, make it harder to try cases well.  Hoffman, Foreword to Case Management report, supra note 7, at vii.  Many judges and others involved in judicial administration have pointed to the positive correlation between the speed and the cost of litigation:  the longer the disposition time of a case, the costlier the litigation becomes--for the parties and for the court.  See, e.g., Case Management report, supra note 7, at 70.  See generally A.L. Levin & E.A. Woolley, Dispatch and Delay:  A Field Study of Judicial Administration in Pennsylvania (1961).

13.  As indicated by the statistics below, the 24 metropolitan federal courts have shown steady improvement in this area over the past decade.  In spite of this improvement, however, the disparity between the fastest and the slowest metropolitan courts continues to be quite wide:

| '77 | '76 | '75 | '74 | '73 | '72 | '71 | '70 | '69 | '68 |
|-----|-----|-----|-----|-----|-----|-----|-----|-----|-----|

Median disposition time for civil cases
in metropolitan courts (months)

| 8 | 9 | 9 | 9 | 9 | 9 | 9 | 10 | 11 | 12 |
|---|---|---|---|---|---|---|----|----|----|

Disparity between fastest and
slowest court (months)

| 21 | 19 | 15 | 14 | 21 | 15 | 20 | 29 | 30 | 26 |
|----|----|----|----|----|----|----|----|----|----|

Source:  Administrative Off. U.S. Courts Ann. Rep.[s] of Dir., table C-5 (1968-1977).

14.  See Curran, table 6.2, at 229, and The Public Image, tables II.5 & II.6, at 19-20, supra note 11.

15.  See Case Management report, supra note 7, at ix-x.

16.  Id. at ix, 25-29.

## Case Populations

Total Case Sample:   the 3,114 cases randomly selected in the six courts.

Discovered Cases:   cases containing at least one discovery request, discovery response, or discovery-related motion.

Completed Cases:   discovered cases in which the parties completed all their discovery, as indicated by the holding of a final pretrial conference or the setting or holding of a trial.

## Events

Discovery Initiatives:   all requests for discovery, motions to limit discovery, motions to compel discovery, and motions for sanctions.

Discovery Requests:   devices provided by the federal rules to secure information; interrogatories (rule 33), depositions (rule 30), requests for documents and things (rule 34), admissions requests (rule 36), subpoenas duces tecum (rule 45(d)), written questions (rule 31), and motions for physical or mental examination (rule 35).

Discovery Responses:   objections or answers to interrogatories, holding of depositions, furnishing material or objections to requests for documents or things, admissions or denials of requests for admissions, the appearance of a nonparty under subpoena, answers or objections to written questions, and answers to motions for physical or mental examinations.

Protecting Motions:   motions to quash (rule 45(b)), motions for protective orders (rule 26(c)), and motions to limit or terminate depositions (rule 30(d)).

Compelling Motions:   motions filed under rule 37(a).

Sanction Motions:   motions filed under rules 37 (a),(b),(c),(d); 41(b); and 55(b) for discovery-related matters.

## Durations

Total Disposition Time:   total amount of time elapsed between filing of the original complaint and entry of the order terminating the case.

Total Discovery Time:   total amount of time elapsed between the filing of the first discovery request and the last response.   If the first request or the last response was not filed by the parties, the first and last recorded initiative or response was used.

Initiation Time:   total amount of time elapsed between the filing of one request and the next.

CHAPTER I

## THE EVOLUTION OF FEDERAL DISCOVERY RIGHTS AND CONTROLS

In order to focus on the ways in which today's district judges handle discovery in civil cases, this chapter provides historical background on the rules governing federal discovery. The first section discusses the reasons for the unification of law and equity under the 1938 rules. Two consequences of this unification had a significant impact on contemporary court procedures: (1) the basis for modern-day discovery was established, and (2) the first opportunity arose for judges to undertake comprehensive management of the civil docket.

The next section of the chapter shows that promulgation of the 1938 rules led to a gradual relaxation of both rule control and the controls given judges over discovery. This trend shifted discovery control to the attorneys.

The final section traces the development of the belief that the contemporary role of the trial judge requires active case management, particularly over discovery in civil cases. As mentioned previously, this report focuses on one judicial control procedure: the use of discovery time controls. The discussion in this chapter poses a question that will be examined in subsequent chapters: Are the discovery provisions in the federal rules sufficient to ensure prompt completion of discovery, or should discovery time controls, particularly discovery cutoff dates, be invoked under rule 83 to promote speedier discovery and shorter disposition times in civil cases?

### The Winding Path Towards Unification of Law and Equity in 1938

Despite the fact that the federal judicial system is almost two hundred years old, only forty years have passed since the federal litigative process was completely revamped when the Federal Rules of Civil Procedure were adopted in 1938. Promulgation of these rules marked a significant departure from traditional forms of civil practice. The full impact of this event can best be appreciated by tracing the evolution of the rules from their roots in the English model of civil procedure.

In the English judicial system, the courts of law developed separately from equity courts.[17] In a court of law, issues of fact were determined by

---

17. See, e.g., Millar, The Formative Principles of Civil Procedure (pt. 1) 18 Ill. L. Rev. 1 (1923); Millar, The Mechanism of Fact-Discovery: A Study in Comparative Civil Procedure (pt. 2), 32 Ill. L. Rev. 424, 437-52 (1937).

a jury, and all witnesses were required to testify orally. Trial was a battle in which counsel used secrecy and surprise to persuade jurors. Because pretrial discovery was considered antithetical to these courtroom tactics, no discovery tools were available to unearth information about an opponent's claim or defense. Focusing the factual issues was, at that time, the purpose of the pleadings, but that process could be quite convoluted. After a complex and protracted series of denials and admissions in which one misstep by a party could prove fatal to his claim or defense, the pleadings system would gradually reduce the controversy to a single issue of fact to be resolved by the jury.

Although discovery rights were not directly available to a party in a court of law, discovery could be obtained indirectly by filing a "bill of discovery" in equity. However, this ancillary equity proceeding was limited to obtaining evidence that supported the position of the discovering party in the case at law, and discovery could not be secured to obtain facts about an opponent's claim or defense.

In marked contrast to the absence of direct discovery in courts of law, various discovery devices, many of which were adopted from canon law, were available in equity cases. The role of the judge in equity was to ensure acquisition of the information needed to reach a just determination of all factual issues. Yet even in equity courts, litigants could not use discovery devices to collect information about an opponent's position.[18]

The dichotomy between English law and equity governed the rules of practice in the early American federal and state courts. Originally, federal courts were required, in all cases, to conform to the rules of procedure of the forum state.[19] Suits in equity were explicitly exempted from this requirement after Congress delegated equity rule-making power to the Supreme Court in 1792[20] and the first equity rules were promulgated in 1822.[21] The equity rules were modified in 1842[22] and 1912.[23] Thus, federal equity practice was allowed to develop uniformly among the districts.

By contrast, until 1938, cases at law were never governed by uniform rules. Generally, federal courts were required to conform to the procedures of the state in which the court was located.[24] This requirement was

---

18. Pike & Willis, The New Federal Deposition-Discovery Procedure (pts. 1 & 2), 38 Colum. L. Rev. 1179, 1436 (1938).

19. Act of Sept. 29, 1789, ch. 21, § 2, 1 Stat. 73, 93.

20. Act of May 8, 1792, ch. 36, § 2, 1 Stat. 275, 276.

21. 20 U.S. (7 Wheat.) v (1822).

22. 42 U.S. (1 How.) xxxix (1842).

23. 226 U.S. 627, 649 (1912).

24. Act of Sept. 29, 1789, ch. 21, § 2, 1 Stat. 93.

intended to provide a uniform set of state and federal procedural rules for cases at law.

Following this principle, however, led to confusion that lasted for more than a century. The first Judiciary Act[25] did not apply to the states admitted to the Union after 1789;[26] moreover, the act required the federal courts to follow state practices as they existed in 1789. Congress acted twice to deal with the dual problems of the static conformity and the non-applicability of the original act to states admitted after 1789. First, a new Conformity Act was passed in 1828,[27] which required the federal courts, in cases at law, to follow the procedure "then" used in the state in which the federal court sat. Second, in 1842,[28] Congress extended the conformity requirement to states that had been admitted between 1828 and 1842. For states admitted to the Union after 1842, Congress incorporated the conformity principle into each enactment granting statehood.[29]

Two additional problems complicated federal procedure in cases at law. Until 1872, some federal courts were required to conform to outdated state procedure. For example, New York's Field Code, adopted in 1848, was the procedural model adopted in many states, but the federal courts in those jurisdictions were still required to follow the states' preexisting, discarded procedures.[30] Also, the federal courts declined to follow some state procedural rules that impinged on substantive federal law.

Although Congress explicitly granted rule-making power over cases at law to the Supreme Court in 1842,[31] the Court failed to promulgate any rules, and Congress withdrew the Court's power in this area in 1872.[32] Congress directed federal courts to conform their practice "as near as may be" to the current procedures of the state in which the court sat.[33] An apt description of the ensuing chaos is the title of an article written shortly before the Federal Rules of Civil Procedure were promulgated: The Origin of the Conformity Idea, Its Development, the Failure of the Experiment, the Evils Which Resulted Therefrom and the Cure for These

---

25. Act of Sept. 24, 1789, ch. 20, § 1, 1 Stat. 73.

26. 4 Wright & Miller Federal Practice and Procedure § 1002, at 33 (1969).

27. Act of May 19, 1828, ch. 68, § 1, 4 Stat. 278.

28. Act of August 1, 1842, ch. 109, 5 Stat. 499.

29. Wright & Miller, supra note 26.

30. Id. at 36.

31. Act of Aug. 23, 1842, ch. 188, §6, 5 Stat. 516, 518.

32. Act of June 1, 1872, ch. 255, § 5, 17 Stat. 196, 197.

33. Id.

Evils.[34]  The proposed "cure" was the adoption of uniform federal procedural rules applicable to cases in both law and equity.

As early as 1911, the American Bar Association urged that Congress
authorize the Supreme Court to promulgate rules to provide a uniform system
of federal procedure.  After obtaining congressional authorization in
1934,[35] the Supreme Court appointed an advisory committee[36] to draft uni-
fied rules applicable to cases at both law and equity.  The Court adopted
the Federal Rules of Civil Procedure on December 20, 1937 (the rules became
effective September 16, 1938),[37] and thereby established the basic frame-
work of contemporary federal discovery.

Key elements of the new rules were the merger of law and equity and
the creation of discovery rules largely patterned after those of the 1912
equity rules.  Discovery tools that previously were only available indirectly, through equity, were now directly available in cases at law.  Under
this new model, pretrial "issue focusing," formerly the role of the pleadings, was shifted to discovery; pleadings were relegated to the less significant role of notifying the parties of the claim or defense.

The combination of simplified pleading and extensive discovery was
intended to expedite dispositions and enhance the ability of the finder of
fact (whether judge or jury) to arrive at the truth of a claim or defense.[38]  No longer were secrecy and surprise appropriate in determining
the outcome of a case.  The drafters of the new rules were convinced that
the search for truth would be better served by a full development of all
the facts prior to presentation at trial.

The spirit underlying the 1938 discovery rules was described by the
Supreme Court in Hickman v. Taylor,[39] in which the Court declared that the
new federal discovery rules were to be "accorded a broad and liberal treatment.  No longer [could] the time-honored cry of 'fishing expedition' serve
to preclude a party from inquiring into the facts underlying his opponent's
case."[40]  Consistent with this new spirit of disclosure, the attorneys were

---

34.  Tolman, 23 A.B.A.J. 971 (1937).  See generally Wright & Miller, supra
note 26, at 31-39; J. Weinstein, Reform of Court Rule-Making Procedures
64-69 (1977).

35.  Act of June 19, 1934, ch. 651, 48 Stat. 1064 (current version at 28
U.S.C. § 2072 (1970).

36.  295 U.S. 774, 774-75 (1935).

37.  Wright & Miller, supra note 26, § 1004, at 49-51.

38.  See generally 4 Moore's Federal Practice ¶26.02, at 26-61 (2d ed.
1976); see also Pike & Willis, supra note 18.

39.  329 U.S. 495 (1947).

40.  Id. at 507.

given increased discretion in shaping their discovery. Subsequent amendments to the rules have continued this trend.

## Shift in the Locus of Control Over Discovery

Tracing the changes in the new rules of discovery from the 1912 Rules of Equity to the 1970 amendments illustrates two trends: (1) expansion of the scope of discovery and (2) relaxation of controls over the frequency and timing of discovery requests. Tables 1 and 2 provide a summary of these trends.

The 1912 equity rules severely restricted discovery, even though discovery was more attainable in equity than in law. Those rules either imposed fixed limitations or gave discretion to the trial judge. The extent of control varied according to the discovery device: for oral depositions and document requests, the judge determined whether there was "good cause" and whether the request had been timely filed; judge approval was not necessary for interrogatories and admissions requests, but the rules limited their frequency and timing.

Under the 1938 rules, discovery was no longer limited to obtaining information about the requesting party's own claim or defense; information could be obtained about an opponent's position as well. The standard for using most discovery devices was also changed: "relevancy to the subject matter" replaced "materiality." Requests for admissions were no longer used solely for issues of authenticity; the 1938 rules permitted admissions of any relevant fact.

The new rules also relaxed control over some discovery devices. Prior judicial approval of the use of oral depositions was no longer required, and parties could notice any number of depositions. Further, the party requesting admissions was no longer limited to one set; the attorney also determined when to file the request, and the judge had no control over that decision unless the party of whom the request was made (the requested party) sought a protective order or the requesting party filed a motion to compel. The process of obtaining information by interrogatories also was changed. Although the rules still limited interrogatories to one set per party,[41] they removed the time limit that had governed how late in the case interrogatories could be filed. Similarly, although the judge still set the time for responses to document requests, the party filing a notice of deposition--not the judge--was made responsible for setting a "reasonable" time for the deposition.

In keeping with this trend toward relaxing the rule restrictions, the decision whether and when to file a motion to compel was left to the party requesting discovery. The sole exception to this policy was for interrogatories. To bring interrogatory disputes to the court's attention, the

---

41. Court approval was required to file more than one set.

party responding to the interrogatories could file objections that would trigger a ruling by the judge on the propriety of the interrogatories. However, if the objections or answers were not timely filed, the burden remained with the initiating party to move the court for an order compelling answers.

The 1946 and 1970 amendments further restricted the judge's control over discovery. The one-set limit for interrogatories was lifted in 1946; thereafter, the parties could file any number of sets. In 1970, the requirement of prior judicial approval of document requests was removed, and the judge no longer ruled directly on objections to interrogatories. Rather, if objections were filed, the requesting party was given the option of moving for a court order to compel the response.

The preceding analysis has shown that changes in the federal discovery rules have gradually given the attorneys virtually unlimited discretion over the initiation of discovery and the enforcement of discovery rights. Of the various types of discovery devices, the rules presently require the court's direct involvement only in motions for mental or physical examination.[42] The rules now allow the attorneys to decide whether and when to file requests[43] and to determine the sequence[44] and frequency[45] of filing. If a response is late or inadequate, or if the request is objected to, the initiating party has the option of moving for a response. Today's rules confer no express authority on judges either to control the initiation of discovery or to require compliance with the time limits set by the rules. Under the present rules, judicial involvement in the discovery process is almost totally dependent on the adversaries.

## Return of Judicial Control Over Discovery

Before 1938, the civil docket of a federal judge had been subject to both federal and state rules of procedure. Equity cases were subject to federal rules, uniformly applicable in each judicial district; cases of law, on the other hand, had been subject to the rules of procedure of each district's forum state (with the exception of some state provisions inimical to federal policy). Thus, the management of a pre-1938 civil docket was subject to potentially antagonistic influences: federal policy might

---

42. These motions, however, account for only a small percentage of the total number of discovery requests filed in federal courts. See fig. 1, infra.

43. None of the rules limit how early in the case a request can be filed. But see Fed. R. Civ. P. 29 (allows modification of the procedures, but allows no extension of response time without court approval).

44. Id. 26(d).

45. Id. 26(a).

# TABLE 1

## DEVELOPMENT OF FEDERAL DISCOVERY RIGHTS

(1) Availability
(2) Ground(s) for Invocation
(3) Purpose
NC  No Change in the Rules

| | Interrogatory | Request for Production of Documents | Request for Admissions | Oral Deposition |
|---|---|---|---|---|
| Pre-1912 equity rules | Law: (1) Unavailable unless forum state so permitted or bill of discovery filed Equity: (1) Available with each pleading only (2) Materiality to issues raised by pleadings (3) Focusing issues only | Law: (1) Unavailable unless forum state so permitted Equity: (1) Unavailable | Law: (1) Unavailable unless forum state so permitted or bill of discovery filed Equity: (1) Available as interrogatory tied to each pleading (2) Materiality (3) Focusing issues only | Law: (1) Any number allowed by statute Equity: (1) Available by statute (2) Absence of witness at trial (3) Preserving testimony for trial |
| 1912 equity rules | Law: (1) NC Equity: (1) One set only (2) NC (3) NC | Law: (1) Unavailable unless forum state so permitted or bill of discovery filed Equity: (1) Available by leave of court | Law: (1) NC (2) Genuineness of documents (3) Elimination of authentication issue at trial | Law: (1) Any number allowed by statute or through a bill of discovery Equity: (1) Available by statute or by rule (2) NC (3) NC |
| 1938 Fed.R.Civ.P. | Law or Equity: (1) One set per party (2) Relevancy under rule 26 (3) Full discovery | Law or Equity: (1) Any number of requests by leave of court (2) Good cause and relevancy under rule 26 (3) Full discovery and gathering evidence for trial | Law or Equity: (1) Any number (2) Relevancy under rule 26 (3) Full discovery and elimination of uncontested authentication issue at trial | Law or Equity: (1) Any number (2) Relevancy under rule 26 (3) Full discovery; preserving testimony at trial; impeaching evidence at trial |
| 1946 amendments | (1) Any number of sets (2) NC (3) NC | (1) NC (2) NC (3) NC | (1) NC (2) NC (3) NC | (1) NC (2) NC (3) NC |
| 1970 amendments | (1) NC (2) NC (3) NC | (1) Any number without need to obtain leave of court (2) Relevancy under rule 26 (3) NC | (1) NC (2) NC (3) NC | (1) NC (2) NC (3) NC |

TABLE 2

DEVELOPMENT OF CONTROLS OVER FEDERAL DISCOVERY RIGHTS

(1) Frequency of Filing or Notice
(2) Time of Filing or Notice
(3) Time of Response
(4) Compelling Response
    A.  Time of Filing
    B.  Process Available

| | Interrogatory | Request for Production of Documents | Request for Admissions | Oral Deposition |
|---|---|---|---|---|
| Pre-1912 equity rules | (1) Fileable with each pleading<br>(2) Time of pleadings governed by the rules<br>(3) Time of pleadings governed by the rules<br>(4) A. No time limit<br>    B. Dismissal or default | No right existed | (1) Fileable with each pleading<br>(2) Time of pleadings governed by the rules<br>(3) Time of pleadings governed by the rules<br>(4) A. No time limit<br>    B. Dismissal or default | (1) Frequency determined by court<br>(2) Time limit set by court<br>(3) Response time set by court<br>(4) A. No time limit<br>    B. Sanctions were dismissal or default |
| 1912 equity rules | (1) One set only[a]<br>(2) Plaintiff or defendant could file at any time up to 21 days after joinder of issue[b]<br>(3) Objections 10 days after filing; Answers 15 days after filing but deferral of all answers until ruling on objections<br>(4) A. No time limit<br>    B. Court ruling on objections, or motion to compel followed by sanctions if court order violated | (1) Court limited frequency<br>(2) Court determined time limit but required to be within pretrial time prescribed by rules<br>(3) Response time set by court<br>(4) A. No time limit<br>    B. Sanctions if failure to answer for violation of court order | (1) One set only<br>(2) Within 10 days before trial<br>(3) 5 days to deny; otherwise deemed admitted<br>(4) A. No time limit<br>    B. Cost of proof at trial borne by requested party | (1) NC<br>(2) For plaintiff, within 60 days of issue; for defendant, within 90 days of issue; rebutting deposition within 20 days of above deadlines<br>(3) NC<br>(4) NC |
| 1938 Fed.R.Civ.P. | (1) NC<br>(2) No time limits[b]<br>(3) NC<br>(4) NC | (1) NC<br>(2) Court determined time limit<br>(3) NC<br>(4) NC | (1) No limit to frequency of filings<br>(2) After close of pleadings<br>(3) 10 days to deny; otherwise deemed admitted<br>(4) A. No time limit<br>    B. Motion to compel denial with particularity for general denials; deemed admitted if no denial; sanctions available under rule 37 if court order violated | (1) No limit to frequency of notices<br>(2) No time limit in rules[b]<br>(3) "Reasonable" time<br>(4) A. No time limit<br>    B. Motion to compel attendance; sanctions under rule 37; protective orders available to deposed party or witness |

[a] Could be exempted by leave of court.
[b] Time limits were set by rule governing filing soon after commencement of action.

| | Interrogatory | Request for Production of Documents | Request for Admissions | Oral Deposition |
|---|---|---|---|---|
| 1946 amendments | (1) No limit to frequency of filings<br>(2) NC<br>(3) Objections 10 days after filing; answers 15 days after filing but with no deferral of answers when objections filed<br>(4) NC | (1) NC<br>(2) NC<br>(3) NC<br>(4) NC | (1) NC<br>(2) From 10 days after commencement of action<br>(3) NC<br>(4) NC | (1) NC<br>(2) NC<br>(3) NC<br>(4) NC |
| 1970 amendments | (1) NC<br>(2) NC<br>(3) Objections and answers to be filed together 30 days after filing of interrogatories<br>(4) A. No time limit<br>B. Motion to compel must be filed for court to rule on objections, inadequate answers, or no answers; sanctions under rule 37 if court order violated or for lateness | (1) No frequency limit in rules<br>(2) No time limits[c]<br>(3) 30 days or shorter<br>(4) A. No time limit<br>B. Motion to compel for nonproduction or inadequate production; sanctions under rule 37 if court order violated or for lateness | (1) NC<br>(2) No time limits[c]<br>(3) 30 days to deny or deemed admitted<br>(4) NC | (1) NC<br>(2) NC<br>(3) NC<br>(4) NC |

[c]A defendant cannot be required to respond before the expiration of 45 days after service of process.

have called for fairly active judicial control of the equity docket, but the forum state's procedural policy might have required a more passive management strategy for the law docket. The unification of federal law and equity courts in 1938 offered the first chance for the federal trial judge to develop a single case management philosophy for the whole civil docket. This unification took place only 40 years ago, nearly 150 years after the establishment of the federal judicial system; consequently, it is hardly surprising that the need for case management procedures only recently has been appreciated.

The relaxation of discovery controls has generated a question whether the mandate of rule 1--the just, speedy, and inexpensive determination of every action--is threatened by reliance solely on the provisions of the federal discovery rules. Judges and legal commentators have taken various approaches in dealing with this perceived "control vacuum."

The role of the judge in the litigative process has been viewed in opposite ways. The "traditional" school of thought has held that the role of the judge is to sit as an umpire in a case, and that expediting litigation, and presumably discovery, is mainly the attorneys' responsibility.[46] The emerging, "activist" school of thought holds that the trial judge must actively supervise each stage of the case to minimize delay. As the following analysis indicates, the activist school of judicial case management has gained increasing support in recent years.

The clarion call to rethink the traditional role of the judge came well in advance of the 1938 rules; in 1906 Dean Roscoe Pound made his famous address, "The Causes of Popular Dissatisfaction With the Administration of Justice," in which he questioned the assumption that a judge should be a "mere umpire."[47] The late Justice Tom C. Clark called that address the spark that lit the "white flame of progress."[48]

The unification of law and equity in 1938 put the judge in the "driver's seat" for the entire civil docket and laid the groundwork for the transformation of the federal judge into an active case manager. The activist school received a boost in 1951 from the report of a committee of five circuit and five district judges, appointed by the late Chief Justice Fred M. Vinson and chaired by Judge E. Barrett Prettyman.[49] The Prettyman re-

---

46. See, e.g., Furstenau, Litigation Management: A Shared Responsibility of the Court and the Bar, 1974 Ariz. St. L.J. 607 (1974).

47. Reprinted in Proceedings in Commemoration of the Address Delivered in St. Paul, Minnesota, August 26, 1906, by Dean Roscoe Pound, 35 F.R.D. 241, 273, 281 (1964).

48. Address by the Honorable Tom C. Clark, id. at 254 (quoting Dean John H. Wigmore).

49. Procedure in Anti-Trust and Other Protracted Cases in "Short Cuts" in Long Cases, 13 F.R.D. 41, 62 (1951).

port, which was adopted by the Judicial Conference of the United States in 1951, recommended special procedures for handling antitrust and other protracted cases--procedures whose implementation assumed active judicial case management:

> The problem of unnecessary delay, volume and expense in these trials [of antitrust and other protracted cases] is much the same as is the problem of efficiency in any undertaking in which numbers of people and masses of material are involved. . . .
> The person who must insure that a case of this nature is thoroughly prepared prior to the trial is the trial judge himself.[50]

In 1963, the Manual for Complex and Multidistrict Litigation[51] recommended various techniques a trial judge could use in processing complex cases. The manual, like the handbook it superseded,[52] recommended techniques that required the judge to take an active role in managing the litigation.

Some judges viewed the case manager role as necessary not only in complex cases, but in routine cases as well.[53]

> I believe that it is impossible to consider seriously the vital elements of a fair trial without concluding that it is the duty of the judge, and the judge alone, as the sole representative of the public interest, to step in at any stage of the litigation where his intervention is necessary in the interest of justice.[54]

The Federal Judicial Center, in keeping with its congressional mandate "to further the development and adoption of improved judicial administration in the courts of the United States,"[55] has conducted seminars for newly appointed district judges, drawing upon the experiences of skilled trial judges and other professionals in the field of judicial administration. The case management procedures advanced at the Center seminars[56] have continued to challenge the assumption that only the lawyers, not the judge,

---

50. Id. at 65.

51. Manual for Complex and Multidistrict Litigation (1963).

52. Handbook of Recommended Procedures for the Trial of Protracted Cases, 25 F.R.D. 351 (1960).

53. See, e.g., Murrah, The Pretrial Conference: Conceptions and Misconceptions, 44 A.B.A.J. 39, 40 (1958).

54. Kaufman, supra note 1, at 216.

55. 28 U.S.C. § 620(a) (1970).

56. See, e.g., Federal Judicial Center, Seminars for Newly Appointed United States District Judges (West Pub. Co. 1970 & 1971; 1973, 1974,

should control the progress of a case.

In addition to this support within the federal judiciary, rules, cases, and statutes also bolster the judge's position as an active case manager. These provisions allow the federal judge to actively supervise the case when the attorneys delay litigation. Under rules 37 and 41(a), the judge has broad powers to sanction delays in discovery or in other phases of the case. This power can be exercised on motion of the parties or, under prevailing case law,[57] it can be initiated by the judge under the inherent power doctrine. Under rule 16, the judge can monitor and supervise the conduct of the case to ensure that the litigation is expedited. A statement by the late Judge Alfred P. Murrah has often been quoted by those who encourage judicial control:

> While the case is in the hands of the lawyers before it has been filed in court, it is their business--but after it reaches the court, it is the public's business, and it is the duty of all to see that it is moved along to final disposition.[58]

In addition, by statute, a judge may order any attorney who "so multiplies the proceedings in any case as to increase costs unreasonably and vexatiously . . . to satisfy personally such excess costs."[59]

_____

1975); Federal Judicial Center, Seminar for Newly Appointed United States District Judges: September 13-18, 1976 (West Pub. Co.); Federal Judicial Center Handbook: Reports and Papers from a Series of Seminars for Seasoned District Judges (West Pub. Co. 1974). See also Comm. on Pretrial Procedure, Judicial Conference of the United States, Seminars for Newly Appointed Judges (West Pub. Co. 1962). Many of the principles enunciated over the years by judges at seminars were evaluated in the Case Management report, supra note 7.

57. In Link v. Wabash R.R., 370 U.S. 626 (1962), the Supreme Court held that a court, in the exercise of its inherent power, may dismiss a case sua sponte, pursuant to Fed. R. Civ. P. 41(b). The Court upheld the right of a district court to dismiss, on its own motion, an action for failure to prosecute, notwithstanding the provision of rule 41(b) that permits dismissal only upon defendant's motion. The inherent power doctrine was recently considered in Van Bronkhorst v. Safera Corp., 529 F.2d 943 (9th Cir. 1976). The Equal Employment Opportunity Commission, an intervenor in a Title VII class action suit, was dismissed with prejudice, inter alia, pursuant to Fed. R. Civ. P. 41(b), for failure to respond to a show-cause order.

58. Kaufman, Discovery, Motions and the Pretrial Conference in Federal Judicial Center, Seminars for Newly Appointed United States District Judges 27, 30 (West Pub. Co. 1963), quoting Judge Murrah. See also, Aldisert, A Metropolitan Court Conquers Its Backlog, Part II: From Pure Pre-trial to Compulsory Settlement Conferences in Judicial Administration 217 (R. Wheeler & H. Whitcomb eds. 1977).

59. 28 U.S.C. § 1927 (1970). In United States v. Ross, 535 F.2d 346 (6th Cir. 1976), the district court's imposition of costs under section 1927 was reversed because the attorney's conduct had been the result of "inadvertent

But no doubt the strongest support for active judicial case management is rule 83. It confers upon courts and judges the discretion to promulgate rules and otherwise regulate federal practice in any manner "not inconsistent with" the Federal Rules of Civil Procedure.

Employing this power to issue standing orders and local rules, some federal judges--and indeed some whole districts--have shifted the locus of control over discovery back to the judge by setting a maximum limit on the time in which the parties can discover.[60] The parties still control the content of their requests (subject to rule 26(b)), and it is within their discretion to select the types of requests as well as the number used and the sequence of their service on opponents. Discovery time controls regulate only the total amount of time allowed for discovery. The two circuits that have considered the validity of such controls have ruled that their use is a valid exercise of judicial power.[61]

As mentioned previously, rule 37 does provide the tools with which to compel timely responses to discovery requests and sanction those who violate the rule provisions. The following chapter will examine how the bar and the bench use rule 37.

---

or negligent acts." Because the conduct was found to be neither "purposeful or malicious" nor "intentional or reckless," there was no basis for imposing sanctions under the statute. Id. at 350-51.

60. One of the first indications of this shift in control philosophy was found in the Manual for Complex and Multidistrict Litigation when it was first adopted in 1963. The handbook that preceded the manual by three years, supra note 52, had not opposed general orders staying discovery. The manual called such orders "unwise," and recommended the use of schedules for the early commencement and completion of discovery. The authors of the manual apparently felt this difference in policies to be of such substantial importance that they cited it as the example of practices in the handbook that were no longer recommended. Manual for Complex Litigation 3 & n.3 (West Pub. Co. 1977).

61. Greyhound Lines, Inc. v. Miller, 402 F.2d 134, 144-45 (8th Cir. 1968); Freehill v. Lewis, 355 F.2d 46, 48 (4th Cir. 1966).

CHAPTER II

## THE USE OF RULE 37 TO DISPATCH DISCOVERY

We have seen that the Federal Rules of Civil Procedure contain no express provisions to limit the timing for initiation or completion of discovery. Rule 37, however, does provide mechanisms for enforcing compliance with discovery requests, through either compelling orders for failure to respond or sanctions for unjustified resistance or inadequate response. The threat of judicial intervention under rule 37 could have a significant impact on timeliness of responses to discovery requests. Such an impact could only be realized, however, if requesting attorneys are reasonably prompt and reasonably consistent in seeking enforcement action from the courts.

### The Compelling Process

The data in Table 3 indicate that the provisions of rule 37 are not an adequate deterrent to dilatory response by the requested party.

TABLE 3
DURATIONS OF RESPONSES TO INTERROGATORIES AND DOCUMENT REQUESTS

| Elapsed Time Between Requests and Responses (Days) | Interrogatories (N=1712) | | Document Requests (N=309) | |
|---|---|---|---|---|
| | No. | % | No. | % |
| 0-30 | 316 | (18.5) | 121 | (39.2)[a] |
| 31-60 | 437 | (27.6)[a] | 111 | (35.9)[a] |
| 61-90 | 338 | (19.7)[a] | 32 | (10.4) |
| 91-120 | 183 | (10.7) | 13 | (4.2) |
| 121-150 | 115 | (6.7) | 7 | (2.3) |
| 151-180 | 63 | (3.7) | 5 | (1.7) |
| 181-210 | 51 | (3.0) | 3 | (1.0) |
| 211-240 | 45 | (2.6) | 4 | (1.3) |
| 241-270 | 26 | (1.5) | 3 | (1.0) |
| 271-300 | 21 | (1.2) | 1 | (0.3) |
| 301-330 | 19 | (1.1) | 1 | (0.3) |
| 331-360 | 8 | (0.5) | -- | -- |
| Over 360 | 55 | (3.2) | 8 | (2.6) |

[a]Denotes median response.

Over 80 percent of responses to interrogatories were filed more than thirty days after requested, and more than 60 percent of responses to document requests exceeded the thirty-day provision. Substantial tardiness appears to be the norm rather than the exception. The median time for

18

response to interrogatories fell in the 61- to 90-day interval, and more than 3 percent of the responses required a year. Responses to document requests were more prompt, but still reflected substantial delays.

Table 4 shows that responsibility for delay must be shared by the requesting party. A compelling motion for either failure or inadequacy of response can be sought thirty days after the discovery request, but that is clearly not the practice. Requesting attorneys frequently wait a substantial amount of time before resorting to rule 37(a).

TABLE 4

COMPELLING MOTIONS BY REQUEST TYPE
AND ELAPSED TIME BETWEEN FILING OF REQUEST
AND FILING OF MOTION

| Elapsed Time (Days) | On Interrogatories (N=391) | | On Document Requests (N=161) | |
|---|---|---|---|---|
| | No. | % | No. | % |
| 0-30 | 25 | (6.4) | 22 | (13.7) |
| 31-60 | 84 | (21.5) | 50 | (31.6) |
| 61-90 | 62 | (15.9) | 33 | (20.5)[a] |
| 91-120 | 56 | (14.3)[a] | 17 | (10.6) |
| 121-150 | 40 | (10.2) | 7 | (4.3) |
| 151-180 | 28 | (7.2) | 6 | (3.7) |
| 181-210 | 25 | (6.4) | 4 | (2.5) |
| 211-240 | 18 | (4.6) | 4 | (2.5) |
| 241-270 | 12 | (3.1) | 2 | (1.2) |
| 271-300 | 11 | (2.8) | 5 | (3.1) |
| 301-330 | 6 | (1.5) | 2 | (1.2) |
| 331-360 | 5 | (1.3) | 2 | (1.2) |
| Over 360 | 19 | (4.9) | 7 | (4.3) |

Note: Two compelling motions in each of the request categories could not be classified.

[a]Denotes the median compelling motion.

The median time between filing an interrogatory and seeking court assistance under rule 37(a) fell in the 91- to 120-day interval; nearly 5 percent of the compelling motions were filed a year after the requests. Again, document requests elicited more prompt reaction from the parties, but that reaction was still far short of the standard contemplated by the rules.

Not only did requesting attorneys wait for substantial periods before filing compelling motions, but in most cases in which responses were late, no motions were ever filed (see table 5).

Only 18 percent of interrogatories unanswered after the passage of thirty days resulted in a rule 37(a) motion. Again, document requests produced greater activity; more than 60 percent of those requests unanswered after thirty days resulted in the filing of compelling motions.

TABLE 5

LATE RESPONSES AND
RULE 37(a) MOTIONS FILED ON TARDINESS GROUNDS

| Request Type | Late Responses[a] | Compelling Motions | |
|---|---|---|---|
| | | No. | % |
| Interrogatory | 1,396 | 254 | (18.2) |
| Document request | 188 | 118 | (62.8) |

[a]This category includes any answer or response filed more than 30 days after the filing of the request for discovery.

Delay in the use of rule 37(a)—or even its nonuse—would be understandable if compelling motions, when used, did not produce the desired results. That was not the situation, however, in the sampled cases, as is shown in table 6.

TABLE 6

COMPELLING MOTIONS, RULINGS, AND GRANTINGS
BY REQUEST TYPE

| Request Type | Compelling Motions | Rulings | | Grantings[a] | |
|---|---|---|---|---|---|
| | | No. | % | No. | % |
| Interrogatory | 254 | 143 | (56.3) | 135 | (94.4) |
| Document request | 118 | 76 | (64.4) | 67 | (88.2) |

[a]This column includes both partially and fully granted motions. There were 134 full grantings for interrogatories and 1 partial; for document requests, there were 64 full and 3 partial.

More than half the compelling motions were ruled upon, and the rulings were overwhelmingly favorable to the moving parties. Although a substantial number of motions were not ruled upon, the absence of ruling often means that the motion was mooted by the filing of the desired response before the court had a chance to rule.

Other data available from the study reveal that such "spontaneous" responses occurred in 31 percent of the compelling motions addressed to interrogatories and 6 percent of those addressed to document requests. The combination of rulings and spontaneous responses demonstrates that substantial adherence to the thirty-day rule could be achieved if attorneys regularly and promptly used the procedures available to them. When given the opportunity, judges seldom found justification for failure to respond. Moreover, the requested party appears to take the very filing of a motion as a sufficiently strong indicator of the requesting party's resolve to produce a response without a court ruling.

A judicial order for a response on a day certain did not, of course, always produce strict compliance with that schedule. Late responses were received in 48 of the 100 instances in which the court ordered an answer to interrogatories and set a date for the response.

Judicial reluctance to enforce rule 37(a) does not explain the failure of the rule to achieve timely filing. The root of the problem lies in the reluctance of requesting parties in many cases to seek court assistance, thereby diluting the effect of the rule as a general deterrent to dilatory response. Another cause of the problem is the tendency of requesting parties, even when they decide to seek assistance, to act as slowly as the requested parties.

## The Sanction Process

Though the compelling process provided by rule 37(a) is not adequately used by attorneys to ensure timely responses to discovery requests, there remains a possibility that the sanction provisions of the rule could constitute a sufficient deterrent to dilatory conduct, if they were used frequently enough to create a substantial risk of punishment for failure to make discovery.

Criticism of the sanction component of rule 37 was voiced in the 1950s,[62] but an analysis of its malfunction was not documented until the Columbia Project for Effective Justice reported its findings to the Advisory Committee on Civil Rules in the early 1960s.[63] That field study reported that parties seldom sought sanctions for opponents' abuses in discovery.[64] When asked the reason for their reticence, attorneys stated that judges imposed sanctions so seldom that filing a motion was usually not worth the time or expense.[65] Concluding that this reluctance threatened the effectiveness of the discovery process, the report recommended revising rule 37.[66]

Substantial amendments to the sanction provisions of rule 37 were made in 1970.[67] To induce more use of the mechanism by attorneys, rule 37(a)(4)

---

62. Rosenberg, Sanctions to Effectuate Pretrial Discovery, 58 Colum. L. Rev. 480, 494-96 (1958). See also Developments in the Law--Discovery, 74 Harv. L. Rev. 940, 990-91 (1961).

63. Glaser report, supra note 6.

64. Id. at 154-56.

65. Id. at 155-56.

66. Id. at 233-45.

67. Amended March 30, 1970, effective July 1, 1970. See generally Proposed Amendments to the Federal Rules of Civil Procedure Relating to Discovery, 48 F.R.D. 487, 539 (1970).

was amended to provide for the award of expenses in seeking or defending a motion compelling discovery, unless the conduct of the opponent was substantially justified or other circumstances would make the award unjust.[68] Also, rule 37(d) cleared up confusion in the case law by expressly making negligent failures to provide discovery--not just willful refusals--sanctionable conduct.[69] To reduce judicial reluctance in sanctioning less egregious discovery abuses, rule 37(b) was amended to allow the award of expenses incurred by parties because of the failure of an opponent to obey a discovery order. This more lenient sanction was added to the stringent measures of dismissal, default, contempt, and others already part of the judicial arsenal.[70] Similarly, rule 37(d) was amended to give the judge power to make "just" orders for a failure to make discovery.[71]

In spite of these efforts, skepticism has been expressed at the prospect that the amendments will make judges less reluctant to impose sanctions.[72] Recent guidance from the Supreme Court[73] may have removed some uncertainty over whether rule 37 could be used by judges to deter noncompliance rather than just to make the moving party whole. That uncertainty may have impeded full use of the judicial powers to sanction discovery abuses.[74] The Committee on Rules of Practice and Procedure, following a recommendation of a special American Bar Association committee,[75] recently recommended that rule 37(e) be amended to authorize judges to sanction those who make unreasonable discovery demands and to impose "such sanctions as are just" without the need for a motion filed by a party.[76]

---

68. Id. at 539.

69. Id. at 541-42.

70. Id. at 540-41.

71. Id. at 541.

72. Before the 1970 amendments became effective, one noted proceduralist said he doubted that the amendment to rule 37(a) would "seriously change the reluctance of courts to impose sanctions. . . ." C. Wright, Law of Federal Courts § 90 (1970).

73. National Hockey League v. Metropolitan Hockey Club, Inc., 427 U.S. 639 (1976).

74. See Note, The Emerging Deterrence Orientation in the Imposition of Discovery Sanctions, 91 Harv. L. Rev. 1033 (1978). The article reports that National Hockey League advised judges that "indulgence of discovery abuses and the narrowly remedial orientation toward discovery sanctions are inappropriate in light of the need to deter all litigants from exploiting the dilatory potential of discovery." Id. at 1034.

75. Section on Litigation, American Bar Ass'n, Report of the Special Committee for the Study of Discovery Abuse 23-25 (1977).

76. Committee on Rules of Practice and Procedure, Judicial Conference of the United States, Preliminary Draft of Proposed Amendments to the Federal

In light of the skepticism voiced about the sanction process, we sought from our data to assess the effects of the rule. The approach, however, had to be different from that used to examine the compelling process.

In examining the compelling process, we could compare the frequency with which attorneys sought compelling orders with the frequency of late responses that would have supported such motions. The sanction provisions of rules 37(b) and 37(d), however, turn upon events not recorded in the court files—primarily the expenses incurred by requesting parties as a result of the requested parties' failure to respond satisfactorily. We have no data to measure the extent of potentially sanctionable conduct. Consequently, we are unable to measure actual requests for sanctions against those that might have been sought.

Even so, we examined the recorded motions for sanctions to see whether the level of activity was extensive enough to provide an incentive for prompt responses. We discovered early that requests for expenses associated with bringing a motion for a compelling order were usually incorporated in the compelling motion filed under rule 37(a). Separate sanction motions were recorded only when the parties sought sanctions under the provisions of rules 37(b), (c), or (d). Since we have already seen that compelling motions are not brought with sufficient regularity to assure timeliness, we turned to assessment of the recorded motions as evidence of enforcement under the last three subsections of the rule.

To conclude that sanctions offer a real prospect of rule control over the timing of responses, we would have to find that sanction requests were brought fairly frequently and that judicial response was consistent and predictable.

The recorded data immediately laid to rest any possibility that sanction requests could be relied upon to police dilatory responses to discovery requests. Only sixty-seven sanction motions were recorded in our sampled cases, as shown in table 7.

The data in table 7 demonstrate very infrequent filing of separate sanction motions. Because of the small number of requests, the variations in frequency associated with different types of discovery requests present little opportunity for conclusions about the frequency of sanctionable conduct arising from each type. It is worth noting, however, that document requests continued to display the greatest activity, even though the amount was small. The percentage of motions ruled upon is slightly smaller than that seen for compelling motions. This again suggests the possibility that spontaneous responses are prompted by filing of the motions, but because of the small number of rulings and grantings, great caution is required in drawing inferences.

--------------------------------

Rules of Civil Procedure 25-36 (1978).

### TABLE 7
### ANALYSIS OF SANCTION MOTIONS

| Type of Request | Requests[a] | Sanction Motions per Request (Total Motions) | Rulings (% of Motions) | Grantings (% of Rulings) |
|---|---|---|---|---|
| Inter-rogatory | 2,519 | 1 in 57 (44) | 20 (45.5%) | 15 (75.0%) |
| Oral deposition | 3,065 | 1 in 438 (7) | 5 (71.4%) | 5 (100%) |
| Document request | 1,031 | 1 in 64 (16) | 10 (62.5%) | 6 (60.0%) |
| Request for admissions | 400 | -- | -- | -- |
| Written questions | 13 | -- | -- | -- |
| Subpoena duces tecum | 39 | -- | -- | -- |
| Mental/phy-sical exam. | 50 | -- | -- | -- |
| Summary | 7,117 | 1 in 106 (67) | 35 (52.2%) | 26[b] (74.3%) |

[a]This is the total number of discovery requests, whether or not a response was produced by the request.

[b]Of the 26 grantings, three were conditional.

Of the sixty-seven sanction motions recorded, thirty-three were filed after a compelling motion had been granted. These motions were assumed to have been filed pursuant to rule 37(b). Half of these sanction motions were filed within thirty days of the order compelling a response to the discovery request. Most of the remainder were filed within sixty days, but six were delayed for many months. No motions were recorded seeking sanction under rule 37(c).

Sanction motions not filed after a compelling order were deemed to have been filed under rule 37(d). Most of these motions (twenty-two) were directed to interrogatories and were filed at various times, ranging from 30 to 360 days after the requests were filed.

It has been asserted that sanctions are not effective because judges are unwilling to impose sanctions when attorneys seek them. Consequently, the argument goes, lawyers simply do not expend the effort and money to invoke rule 37.[77] The result is certainly demonstrated in the data--

---

77. Glaser report, supra note 6, at 154-56. See also Rosenberg, Sanctions to Effectuate Pretrial Discovery, supra note 62.

lawyers do not often move for sanctions. This information is shown in table 8. It is very difficult to evaluate the putative cause; sixty-seven motions is not a large base from which to assess the attitudes of the federal bench. In the few instances where judges were given an opportunity to impose sanctions, however, the data do not reveal the pervasive hostility that was alleged before the 1970 revisions.

TABLE 8
RULINGS AND GRANTINGS OF
RULE 37(d) AND RULE 37(b) SANCTION MOTIONS

| Motion Type | Number of Motions | Number of Rulings (% of Motions) | Number of Grantings[a] (% of Rulings) |
|---|---|---|---|
| Rule 37(d) | 34 | 11 (32.4%) | 8 (72.8%) |
| Rule 37(b) | 33 | 24 (72.7%) | 18 (75.0%) |
| Summary | 67 | 35 (52.2%) | 26 (74.3%) |

[a]One of the 8 grantings of rule 37(d) sanctions was conditional; 2 of the 18 grantings of rule 37(b) sanctions were conditional.

More than half the motions were ruled upon, and three-quarters of the rulings favored the moving party. If we assume that some portion of the motions without rulings were mooted by a response before the judge had an opportunity to rule, there is a substantial positive response from the use of rule 37. Only nine denials were reported--hardly persuasive evidence that sanction requests fall upon deaf ears.

The infrequent resort to sanction motions leads us to conclude that these provisions of rule 37, as applied by the litigating attorneys, do not constitute an important incentive to prompt discovery response. As observed above, the amount of sanctionable conduct is unknown, but from these data we can draw one of the following inferences:

1. The rarity of sanction motions indicates that very little sanctionable conduct is occurring.

2. Though sanctionable conduct occurs frequently, requesting parties do not seek to punish it by invoking court authority under rule 37.

Whichever may be the true condition prevailing in the courts under study, the data available to us indicate that reliance on court control initiated by the attorneys under any or all of the provisions of rule 37 will be unavailing.[78] The federal rules' lack of express controls over timing,

---

78. Protecting motions would not directly affect timing control, but their

and the demonstrated reluctance of litigating attorneys to enforce prompt responses, have led some courts to establish, under the authority of rule 83, local rules or practices to control the pace of discovery. The effect of those efforts will be examined in chapter five.

---

use may be of interest in appraising the total discovery process. Data on these motions are reported in appendix D.

## CHAPTER III

## QUANTIFYING THE USE OF DISCOVERY

Our exploration to this point has revealed a decided trend toward loosening control of discovery by rule. The rule 37 sanctions for failure to make discovery could affect the timeliness of discovery, because of both the deterrent effect of sanctions and the compelling portion of the rule. This rule and its mechanisms, however, clearly do not achieve system-wide timeliness.

If we are to look outside the rules for controls, we must look to the effectiveness of controls imposed under rule 83. It is important to be aware of the context within which these controls operate. This includes knowing whether all civil cases have discovery and whether there is relative homogeneity or heterogeneity in the types and number of discovery problems among all cases. Common sense and experience tell us there are large differences in the "size" of cases and in the problems they engender, but there have been very few data that describe the extent of these differences in terms of the number of discovery initiatives and the elapsed time for the conduct of all discovery in a case. To that end, in this chapter we explore data of this type to describe the context within which judicial controls can be applied.

The District Court Studies Project collected extensive data on a sample of more than 3,000 cases terminated in six metropolitan courts during fiscal year 1975. The data collected for the project included every discovery event recorded in the court files for the cases. Discovery events are defined in the Glossary (supra); they include discovery requests, responses, and motions in aid of the discovery process.

It was recognized from the outset that not all discovery accomplished by litigating parties would be recorded in court files, despite the requirements of rule 5. To assess how reliably recorded discovery events indicate total discovery activity, we conducted a small survey of lawyers who had appeared in the sample cases. Sixty attorneys (ten from each district) were randomly selected from those appearing in our sample of cases. Telephone interviews with these attorneys revealed that approximately 75 percent of total discovery activity was regularly recorded with the courts.[79] From the responses, we conclude that the recorded data described

---

79. The interview instrument and tabulations of responses are included in appendix C.

in this report provide a reliable basis for the observations and recommendations advanced. There is certainly more discovery being accomplished than is reflected by these data, but the recorded data describe total activity sufficiently to warrant reliance upon them--not only in this report and other parts of the District Court Studies Project, but also in future studies, where capturing data on unrecorded litigation activity may be prohibitively expensive or time-consuming.

## The Extent of Discovery Use

Table 9 shows that approximately 52 percent of the cases in the study sample had no recorded discovery requests. Cases having discovery (discovered cases) ranged from those with only one discovery request (10.5 percent of the total) to a case with sixty-two requests. It is interesting to note that 95.1 percent of the cases had ten or fewer discovery requests.

In order to simplify these data, cases having discovery are grouped into three volume categories as follows:

Low Volume — Those discovered cases having one to three discovery requests

Moderate Volume — Those discovered cases having three to ten requests

High Volume — Those discovered cases having eleven or more requests

Table 10 shows the number and percentage of discovered cases, and the average number of requests per case, for each volume category. Across all three volume categories, there were three requests in the median case, and an average of 4.7 requests per case. It should be emphasized that the overall median and average figures are for discovered cases only--if all cases were considered, both figures would be lower.

The number of requests is a somewhat sterile datum unless we know the types of discovery that are being used. Figure 1 shows the number and proportion of use of each of the seven discovery devices. Depositions and interrogatories are by far the most frequently used. These two devices account for 78.5 percent of the 7,117 discovery requests that were filed in the 3,114 cases comprising the sample. Requests for production of documents, 14.5 percent of the total, and requests for admissions, 5.6 percent of the total, were less frequently used, but had substantial usage compared to the remaining three devices, each of which represented less than 1 percent of total discovery requests.

It is important to know the amount of discovery in those cases in which discovery is completed. Many cases are terminated while discovery is

TABLE 9

NUMBER OF CASES BY NUMBER OF DISCOVERY REQUESTS

| No. of Requests | No. of Cases | Percent of Cases | Cumulated Percent |
|---|---|---|---|
| 0 | 1,610 | 51.7 | 51.7 |
| 1 | 326 | 10.5 | 62.2 |
| 2 | 316 | 10.1 | 72.3 |
| 3 | 213 | 6.8 | 79.2 |
| 4 | 159 | 5.1 | 84.3 |
| 5 | 119 | 3.8 | 88.1 |
| 6 | 72 | 2.3 | 90.4 |
| 7 | 50 | 1.6 | 92.0 |
| 8 | 42 | 1.3 | 93.4 |
| 9 | 28 | 0.9 | 94.3 |
| 10 | 27 | 0.9 | 95.1 |
| 11 | 31 | 1.0 | 96.1 |
| 12 | 18 | 0.6 | 96.7 |
| 13 | 22 | 0.7 | 97.4 |
| 14 | 15 | 0.5 | 97.9 |
| 15 | 7 | 0.2 | 98.1 |
| 16 | 6 | 0.2 | 98.3 |
| 17 | 3 | 0.1 | 98.4 |
| 18 | 8 | 0.3 | 98.7 |
| 19 | 2 | 0.1 | 98.7 |
| 20 | 5 | 0.2 | 98.9 |
| 21 | 1 | 0.0 | 98.9 |
| 22 | 4 | 0.1 | 99.1 |
| 23 | 3 | 0.1 | 99.2 |
| 24 | 2 | 0.1 | 99.2 |
| 25 | 3 | 0.1 | 99.3 |
| 26 | 1 | 0.0 | 99.4 |
| 27 | 2 | 0.1 | 99.4 |
| 28 | 1 | 0.0 | 99.5 |
| 29 | 3 | 0.1 | 99.6 |
| 30 | 1 | 0.0 | 99.6 |
| 31 | 2 | 0.1 | 99.6 |
| 32 | 1 | 0.0 | 99.7 |
| 33 | 2 | 0.1 | 99.7 |
| 34 | 1 | 0.0 | 99.8 |
| 35 | 1 | 0.0 | 99.8 |
| 42 | 1 | 0.0 | 99.8 |
| 43 | 1 | 0.0 | 99.9 |
| 46 | 1 | 0.0 | 99.9 |
| 52 | 1 | 0.0 | 99.9 |
| 53 | 1 | 0.0 | 100.0[a] |
| 62 | 1 | 0.0 | 100.0 |
| | 3,114 | 100.0 | |

[a]This percentage was rounded up to 100.0%.

TABLE 10

ANALYSIS OF DISCOVERY IN DISCOVERED CASES

| Volume Categories | No. Cases | % Cases | Average Requests per Case |
|---|---|---|---|
| Low | 642 | 42.7 | 1.49 |
| Moderate | 710 | 47.2 | 4.94 |
| High | 152 | 10.1 | 17.47 |

FIGURE 1

PROPORTIONS OF REQUEST TYPES FOR DISCOVERED CASES

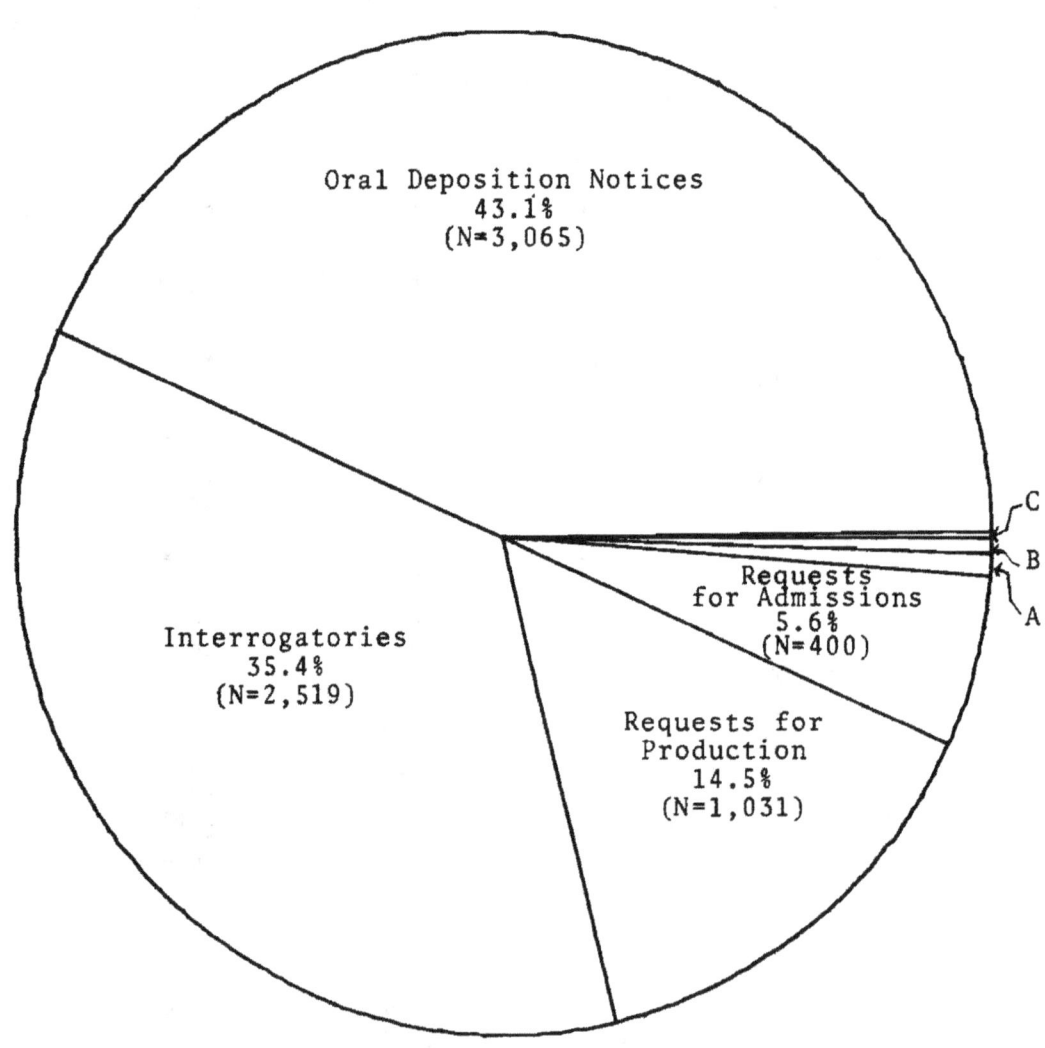

A    Motions for Mental or Physical Examination
         0.7%
         (N=50)

B    Subpoenas Duces Tecum
         0.5%
         (N=39)

C    Written Questions
         0.2%
         (N=13)

still underway, and the data on discovered cases shown above necessarily include these. The data on "completed" cases--cases in which discovery was completed--provide a better measure of what to expect in those cases in which attorneys make substantially all the discovery they need; these cases represent the "expectation potential" for each case at its inception. Completed cases were identified as those in which a final pretrial conference or a trial was held.[80] Table 11 shows volume data for completed cases.

TABLE 11

ANALYSIS OF DISCOVERY IN COMPLETED CASES

| Volume Categories | No. Cases[a] | % Cases | Average Requests per Case |
|---|---|---|---|
| Low | 79 | 19.8 | 1.67 |
| Moderate | 241 | 60.4 | 5.14 |
| High | 79 | 19.8 | 17.46 |

[a]Cases with no discovery requests were excluded from computations shown in this table.

As expected, the overall median and average are higher than for discovered cases: there were five requests in the median case, and an average of 6.9 requests per case. Although the percentage of moderate- and high-volume cases is higher (as would be expected) the amount of discovery for completed high-volume cases is almost exactly the same as the average for all high-volume cases. Only half (79 out of 152)[81] of the high-volume cases completed discovery, yet the average number of requests per case was the same (17.46 versus 17.47), indicating that the probability of high-volume discovery, and the consequent need to manage discovery, is not affected by the probability of settlement.[82]

Table 12, showing the average number of requests and discovery-related

---

80. In Central California and Massachusetts, the holding of a final pretrial conference was inferred from the appearance of a scheduled trial date in the court file. In both of these courts, a trial date was generally set only at the final pretrial conference, but the final pretrial conference was not always recorded.

81. Cf. table 10.

82. Discovery "initiatives" (requests plus discovery-related motions) per completed case were also computed. There were five initiatives in the median completed case and an average of eight per completed case.
    Since the sample of completed cases was controlled for early case terminations, subsequent statistical analysis, whenever possible, will be derived from that population instead of from the discovered population.

motions[83] per completed case, provides a profile of the average case.[84]

TABLE 12

AVERAGE DISCOVERY INITIATIVES PER
COMPLETED CASE
(N=399)

### Requests

| | |
|---|---|
| Notices of deposition . . . . . . . . . . . . . . . . | 3.20 |
| Interrogatories . . . . . . . . . . . . . . . . . | 2.28 |
| Requests for document production . . . . . . . . . | 0.93 |
| Requests for admissions . . . . . . . . . . . . . | 0.34 |
| Motions for physical or mental examinations . . . . | 0.08 |
| Subpoenas duces tecum . . . . . . . . . . . . . . | 0.04 |
| Written questions . . . . . . . . . . . . . . . . | 0.01 |

### Discovery-Related Motions

| | |
|---|---|
| Compelling motions . . . . . . . . . . . . . . . . | 1.38 |
| Protecting motions . . . . . . . . . . . . . . . . | 0.39 |
| Motions for sanctions . . . . . . . . . . . . . . | 0.36 |

As can readily be seen, the average case had about three notices of depositions,[85] two interrogatories, and one request for documents; the remaining types of requests were far less frequently used.

Discovery-related motions punctuated the discovery process. Slightly more than one-third of the completed cases had at least one discovery-related motion filed. Overall, about two such motions were filed per completed case; compelling motions outnumbered both protecting motions and

---

83. Discovery-related motions include motions to compel (compelling motions); motions for sanctions; and motions for protective orders, to limit or terminate depositions, and to quash subpoenas (hereafter referred to as protecting motions).

84. These data are of special importance in setting cutoff dates for discovery. The requests listed in the profile each have a time dimension--the time it takes an opponent to respond. Since response times vary widely by request type, connecting a time to the frequency of requests filed will give a dual perspective for discovery management considerations. For example, answering interrogatories took, on the average, more than three times longer than the duration between noticing and holding of oral depositions (see table 26, infra). In addition, discovery-related motions have a time dimension that must be taken into account in setting a reasonable time for discovery. A forthcoming study in the District Court Studies Project shows the processing of compelling motions averaged 29 days from filing of the motion to the ruling. E. Holleman, Judicial Controls and the Civil Litigative Process: Motions (Federal Judicial Center 1978).

85. The deponents were: parties, 54.2%; doctors, 3.3%; other experts, 4.8%; records custodians, 5.4%; other witnesses, 25.6%; unknown, 6.8%.

motions for sanction by 3 to 1.

Variability in the composition of discovery for completed cases was studied by comparing the average filings for each of the seven request types in each volume category. Because discovery in the high-volume cases had a rather wide range (from a low of eleven to a high of sixty-two requests), that category was divided into three subcategories. Table 13 reports the results.

TABLE 13

AVERAGE REQUESTS PER COMPLETED CASE
BY TYPE AND VOLUME CATEGORY

| | Volume Categories | | | | |
|---|---|---|---|---|---|
| | Low | Moderate | High | | |
| | (1-2) | (3-10) | (11-20) | (21-30) | (31+) |
| Request Types | | | | | |
| Oral deposition notices | .7 | 2.4 | 6.0 | 11.5 | 19.5 |
| Interrogatories | .7 | 1.8 | 6.0 | 7.1 | 10.6 |
| Document requests | .1 | .6 | 2.0 | 4.1 | 7.5 |
| Admission requests | .1 | .2 | .9 | .8 | 2.4 |
| Physical/mental exam. motions | .0 | .0 | .2 | 1.1 | .2 |
| Subpoenas duces tecum | -- | .0 | .1 | .5 | .1 |
| Written questions | .0 | .0 | .1 | -- | -- |
| Summary | 1.6 | 5.0 | 15.3 | 25.1 | 40.3 |

Composition of discovery does vary as the volume of discovery increases. Through the "11-20" volume category, interrogatories and oral deposition notices were filed at equal rates. In the cases with higher discovery volume, however, oral depositions were an increasingly more popular discovery device. This contrast is best illustrated by comparing the ratio of interrogatories to depositions between the two extreme volume categories: in the low-volume cases, it was one to one, but in the "31+" category, there were almost two oral depositions for each interrogatory.

The effect of discovery volume on the filing of discovery-related motions is reflected in the average number of motions filed per discovery request for each of the volume categories (see table 14). The discovered-

case population was used in this analysis because the low numbers of discovery-related motions filed in the completed-case population would not
permit reliable comparisons by volume categories.

TABLE 14

AVERAGE DISCOVERY-RELATED MOTIONS
PER DISCOVERY REQUEST IN DISCOVERED CASES
BY VOLUME CATEGORIES

| Volume Categories | Compelling Motions | Protecting Motions | Sanction Motions | All Discovery-Related Motions |
|---|---|---|---|---|
| Low (N=642) | .07 | .03 | -- | .09[a] |
| Moderate (N=710) | .09 | .03 | .01 | .12[a] |
| High (11-20 requests) (N=21) | .09 | .03 | .01 | .13 |
| High (21-30 requests) (N=13) | .10 | .02 | .00 | .13[a] |
| High (31+ requests) (N=13) | .15 | .05 | .03 | .23 |

[a]Due to rounding error, the average for all discovery-related motions did not correspond to the addition of the averages for each
motion.

The column in table 14 marked "All Discovery-Related Motions" shows
that increasing amounts of discovery resulted in increasing requests for
judicial attention. The differences in average motions per request between the extremes of discovery volume was more than double: .09 to .23.

The increased rate of discovery-related motions was primarily attrib-
utable to increased filings of compelling motions. The table shows that
protecting motions increased in averages only slightly through the volume
categories; motions for sanctions were seldom filed, although the parties
in cases with thirty-one or more requests sought more sanctions.[86] Compelling motions, on the other hand, increased steadily as the volume of total
requests increased.

These increases in average motions per request had a dramatic effect
on the average motions per case (not shown in the table). In the low-
volume cases, only one in every seven cases had a motion filed, compared to
an average of nine motions per case for the average case with thirty-one or

86. On an average, one motion for sanction was filed in each case with
thirty-one or more requests.

more requests.

Counting cases and counting discovery initiatives will not, of course, lay to rest the considerable controversy over operation of discovery under the federal rules.[87] The data presented here, however, do provide a context in which to view the controversy and to assess proposals, including those advanced in this report, for improving the discovery process.

Also, these data do not directly address the question of discovery abuse. It is possible for a single discovery request to be abusive, as it is possible for sixty-two requests to be appropriate, relevant, and facilitative in the just disposition of a particular case. The data do suggest, however, that discovery abuse, to the extent it exists, does not permeate the vast majority of federal filings. In half the filings, there is no discovery--abusive or otherwise. In the remaining half of the filings, abuse--to the extent it exists--must be found in the quality of the discovery requests, not in the quantity, since fewer than 5 percent of the filings involved more than ten requests.

---

87. See Committee on Rules of Practice and Procedure, Judicial Conference of the United States, Preliminary Draft of Proposed Amendments to the Federal Rules of Civil Procedure 6-11 (1978). For expressions of concern about discovery, see Section on Litigation, American Bar Ass'n, Report of the Special Committee for the Study of Discovery Abuse 1-3 (1977). See also Lindquist & Schechter, The New Relevancy: An End to Trial by Ordeal, 64 A.B.A.J. 59 (1978).

CHAPTER IV

## PREDICTING DISCOVERY ACTIVITY

The data examined thus far show that there is considerable variation in the amount of discovery. Most cases, however, are seen to involve very little. For those cases, regularly imposed discovery timing controls should present little difficulty for the attorneys or for the court. The problem is to recognize at an early stage those cases likely to involve extensive discovery activity, so that fair, effective, and realistic schedules can be applied to those cases that need them, while avoiding wasted effort on cases of small volume. In this chapter, therefore, we examine various characteristics of the pleadings to determine how much predictive value they provide to the judge who seeks to control the movement of the discovery process.

Case management can be effectuated by numerous devices. Observation of practices and results in the study courts lead us to suggest that judges should place cases on either a discovery control track or a motions control track, and that the choice can be informed by case characteristics evident in the pleadings. Further, for cases placed on the discovery control track, pleadings characteristics provide early indicators of the amount of discovery, so that the time required for accomplishing discovery can be estimated.

### Selecting a Management Track

Some cases almost never generate issues of fact and are usually terminated by motion. Such cases would not benefit from discovery timing controls. These cases can be identified by the subject matter area disclosed in the original complaint.

In some subject matter areas, the federal statute defining the court's jurisdiction either limits or totally precludes the raising of factual issues. In many appeals from administrative rulings, for example, the district court's jurisdiction is limited to determining the substantiality of evidence supporting the federal agency's findings of fact.[88] Discovery plays little or no role in these cases. Once the issue is joined, disposi-

_____

88. The role of the district court depends on the statute on which the suit is based. A good example is the Coal Mine Health and Safety Act of 1969, 30 U.S.C. §§ 801-878 (as amended) (1970). Under section 819(a)(4) of the act, the district court, after several tiers of review in the admin-

36

tive motions are filed, and the court usually grants one of the motions, terminating the case without any discovery.

Because of the scarcity of discovery in administrative appeals[89] and other areas of litigation, the imposition of timing controls over discovery would more likely delay than advance termination of those cases. Identification of these areas permits the judge to impose management controls consistent with the expectation of termination by motion.

Fifteen areas of litigation most heavily represented in the case sample[90] were examined to determine the proportion of discovered and nondiscovered cases in each area.[91] Figure 2 displays these proportions. Prisoner[92] and administrative appeals cases exhibited the highest proportion of nondiscovered terminations. Similar proportions appeared in seizure cases, Interstate Commerce Commission (ICC) cases, and condemnation cases. Discovered cases in other areas of litigation ranged from 40 to 70 percent.

---

istrative process (except issues of fact litigated in ancillary proceedings), must consider and determine de novo all issues relevant to civil penalties assessed against a coal operator. Under section 818 of the act, the district court must consider civil actions for relief filed by the United States if orders issued through the administrative process are violated. By contrast, under section 923(b) of subchapter IV of the act (30 U.S.C. §§ 901-936 (as amended)), the district court reviews entitlements to black lung benefits based on the "substantial evidence" rule, in much the same way as disability insurance benefits are reviewed under 42 U.S.C. § 423 (1970). Also, under section 816 of the safety provisions of the act, the district court is bypassed completely in the process of reviewing those orders of the administrative agency that do not fall under the purview of sections 818 and 819, and it is the court of appeals that must review, based on "substantial evidence."

89. As the Coal Mine Health and Safety Act illustration (note 88 supra) shows, placing all cases that emanate from administrative proceedings into one category runs the risk of including some cases that raise factual issues to be determined de novo and thus could generate discovery. Nevertheless, for the sake of this analysis, it was assumed that most of these types of cases did not have a de novo provision, and that the bulk of these cases would have no discovery. In chapter seven, the case-tracking system takes into account the possibility that some of these cases will have discovery and will need to be removed from the motions track.

90. Because of low numbers of case filings, some familiar areas of litigation, such as environmental cases, were not represented.

91. The process used to classify the cases by area of litigation is described infra, in "Subject Matter of Controversy."

92. This category included petitions for habeas corpus filed under 28 U.S.C. § 2254 (1970) and motions attacking federal sentences filed under 28 U.S.C. § 2255 (1970). Under both statutes, the scope of judicial review forecloses, in most instances, the raising of factual issues. For analysis purposes, prisoner civil rights suits filed under 42 U.S.C. § 1983 (1970) were included in the prisoner case category. Although discovery on the nature of the alleged constitutional deprivation is not precluded by the statute, these cases were included with the above cases because a substantial majority of them were decided on the pleadings.

FIGURE 2

PROPORTION OF DISCOVERED CASES
AND NONDISCOVERED CASES
BY SELECTED AREAS OF
LITIGATION

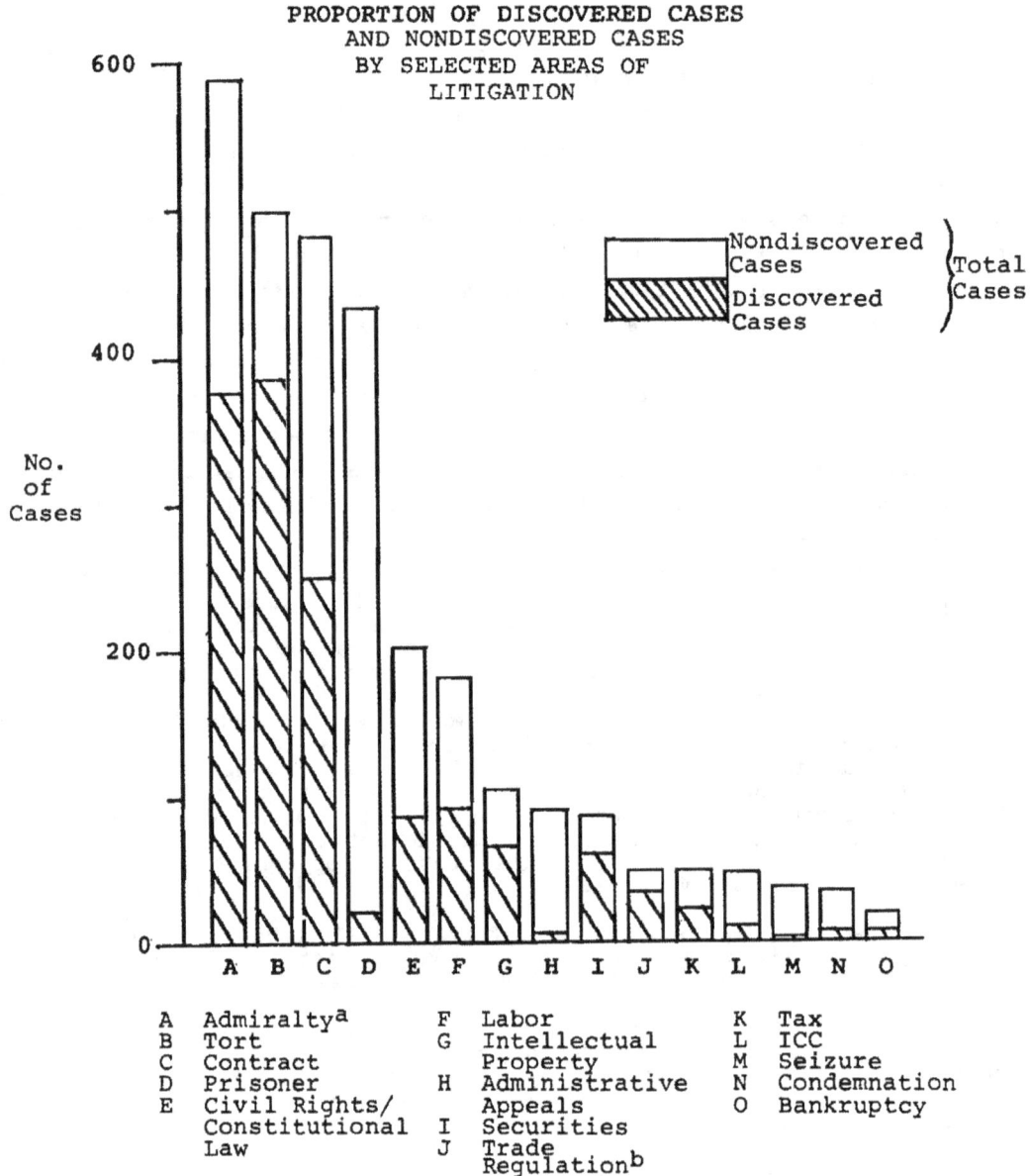

A  Admiralty[a]        F  Labor                K  Tax
B  Tort                G  Intellectual         L  ICC
C  Contract               Property             M  Seizure
D  Prisoner            H  Administrative       N  Condemnation
E  Civil Rights/          Appeals              O  Bankruptcy
   Constitutional      I  Securities
   Law                 J  Trade
                          Regulation[b]

[a]This category includes Jones Act cases.
[b]This category includes antitrust cases.

For these five areas, in which 75 percent or more of the cases were terminated without discovery, the nondiscovered cases were examined to determine whether motion disposition was common where discovery was absent. Table 15 reports the number and percentage of each type of disposition for each of these five areas.

TABLE 15

NONDISCOVERED CASES IN FIVE AREAS OF LITIGATION, BY DISPOSITION

| | Motion | | Settlement | | Voluntary Dismissal | | Trial | |
|---|---|---|---|---|---|---|---|---|
| | No. | % | No. | % | No. | % | No. | % |
| Prisoner cases (N=411) | 378 | (92.0) | 13 | (3.2) | 10 | (2.4) | 10 | (2.4) |
| Admin. appeals (N=98) | 58 | (59.2) | 22 | (22.4) | 15 | (15.3) | 3 | (3.0) |
| Seizure cases (N=34) | 23 | (67.6) | 6 | (17.6) | 1 | (2.9) | 4 | (11.8) |
| ICC cases (N=28) | 12 | (42.9) | 11 | (39.3) | 5 | (17.9) | -- | |
| Condemnation cases (N=27) | 7 | (25.9) | 18 | (66.7) | -- | | 2 | (7.4) |

Prisoner cases, administrative appeals, and seizure cases were characteristically terminated by motion with virtually no discovery. These cases are candidates for management by a special motions track, discussed in chapter seven. Cases in the other two areas are so often disposed of by settlement that they remain candidates for discovery control.

## Factors Affecting Amount of Discovery

For cases likely to have discovery and needing discovery timing control, the judge must decide how much time to allow for discovery. The judge's experience is, of course, the prime asset at this point. Certain characteristics of the case may suggest the probability that little discovery will be needed and that a relatively short discovery period would easily accommodate the parties. On the other hand, other characteristics may earmark the "big" case, which will require a substantial amount of time for discovery. This section is intended to help the judge schedule discovery, by assessing the predictive value of case characteristics identifiable from the pleadings.

Variability in discovery amounts was expected to be related to the nature of each controversy. To assess this relationship, five case-related characteristics of civil controversies were studied.[93] The strength of association between these characteristics and discovery activity provides guidance for predicting the discovery time needed by the parties.[94]

Positive statistical relationships were observed between the following case-related characteristics and the variance in discovery:

1. subject matter of the controversy
2. number of parties
3. presence of a controverted counterclaim
4. presence of a controverted cross claim

The amount in controversy exhibited a slight relationship, but was found to be less reliable as an indicator of discovery use.[95]

The analysis examined the extent to which each characteristic, inde-pendently of all other characteristics, is related to the number of discov-ery requests. In other words, it examined the question, "Are different values of the characteristic related to different amounts of discovery?"[96] An important aspect of the procedure is the independence of each character-istic's contribution to changes in the number of discovery requests.

## Subject Matter of Controversy

Considering the wide range of controversies adjudicable in district courts, the subject matter of the case appeared to be an obvious factor in

---

93. Other factors that might also have contributed to these differences, such as the case management philosophy of the court, the practices of the local federal bar, and the case load of the court, are not addressed be-cause the data do not reveal them.

94. This predicting system is discussed more fully in chapter seven.

95. In all probability, the true value of a controversy would exhibit a high degree of correlation with discovery activity. The only datum avail-able was the amount claimed in the ad damnum clause. The fact that the correlation was weak probably reflects an underlying weak relationship be-tween the prayer and the true value. Accordingly, where more reliable in-dicators signal that there are very substantial amounts in controversy, the judge should be alert to the possibility of increased discovery activity.

96. To provide the judge with some perspective on these values, a paradigm of a discovered case that had none of these characteristics, and which had been subjected to discovery timing controls, is a case with two parties, no pleadings other than a complaint and an answer, and of a type not listed in table 17, infra. That paradigm case averaged 3.4 requests; it forms the base to which could be added the increased requests produced by the pres-ence of each of the four characteristics. Prisoner, administrative ap-peals, and seizure cases were excluded from this and all subsequent calcu-lations in this chapter.

accounting for variations in discovery.[97]

Studying the impact of this factor required classifying the sampled cases in two ways: (1) assigning them to finely graded case types (e.g., admiralty-cargo damage, contracts-warranty, etc.) allowing a focused analysis of cases, and (2) aggregating the case types into broader subject matter areas of federal litigation (e.g., admiralty, contracts, etc.), allowing gross, but more statistically reliable, comparisons.[98]

Table 16 depicts the patterns of discovery use in fifteen subject matter areas of federal litigation. The table shows the percentage of cases at each volume of discovery, the percentage of nondiscovered cases,[99] the median case, and the average requests per case filing and per discovered case. The subject matter areas are ranked in descending order by average requests for all cases.

Table 16 indicates that the subject matter is substantially associated with the amount of discovery filed by the parties. The difference this factor makes is demonstrated in the column showing average requests per case for all cases. For instance, securities and trade regulation cases averaged more than nine times the discovery in condemnation cases and almost twice that in contract cases.

The averages are substantially influenced by the presence of a relatively small number of high-volume cases. This point is apparent from the column showing percentages of high-volume cases. Each of the top eight areas (the labor category and above) had at least one case with high-volume discovery, and most of these areas had several. By contrast, in the bottom seven areas ("Tax" and below),[100] only three cases involved high volume. (Surprisingly, two were prisoner cases.[101])

---

97. The analysis of the nondiscovered cases already showed that in certain subject matter areas like prisoner, administrative appeals, and seizure cases, discovery rarely occurs. Supra, table 15 and accompanying text.

98. Classification systems used by the Administrative Office of the United States Courts (AO) and in the Glaser report, supra note 6, were considered, but neither appeared suitable for this analysis. Two reasons precluded the use of the AO system: (1) Since in most clerk's offices it is the practice to have the attorneys filing the case classify it according to the AO scheme, there was some danger of misclassification; and (2) the categories themselves are not sufficiently precise to study particular areas of litigation, such as product liability and securities. In the Glaser report, the cases were classified by subject matter into only two categories--commercial and personal injury--which were too general for our purposes.

99. This can be obtained by subtracting the cumulated percentage in the "Low" volume column from 100 percent.

100. Three of them have a heavy emphasis on motion practice. See table 15, supra.

101. Both cases were filed in the District of Maryland. The cases were closely related and were filed under 42 U.S.C. § 1983 (1970). One was

TABLE 16

DISCOVERY USE BY AREA OF LITIGATION

| Area of Litigation[a] | Volume Categories | | | | | | Total Cases | Average Requests | |
|---|---|---|---|---|---|---|---|---|---|
| | High | | (11-20) | Moderate (3-10) | Low (1-2) | Non-discovered | | All Case Filings | Discovered Cases |
| | (31+) No. % | (21-30) No. % | No. % | No. % | No. % | No. % | | | |
| Securities | 2 (2.3) | 1 (3.4) | 7 (11.5) | 36 (52.9)c | 15 (70.1) | 26 (100) | 87 | 4.6 | 6.6 |
| Trade regulation | -- | 1 (2.0) | 5 (12.0) | 20 (52.0)c | 9 (70.0) | 15 (100) | 50 | 4.3 | 6.1 |
| Tort | 6 (1.2) | 5 (2.2) | 31 (8.4) | 203 (49.2)c | 140 (77.3)c | 113 (100) | 498 | 4.1 | 5.3 |
| Intellectual property | 1 (0.9) | 5 (5.7) | 6 (11.3) | 24 (34.0) | 31 (63.2)c | 39 (100) | 106 | 3.7 | 5.8 |
| Admiralty[b] | 2 (0.3) | 6 (1.4) | 42 (8.5) | 168 (37.1) | 158 (63.9)c | 212 (100) | 588 | 3.3 | 5.1 |
| Contract | 1 (0.2) | -- | 18 (3.9) | 138 (32.6) | 93 (51.9)c | 232 (100) | 482 | 2.4 | 4.5 |
| Civil rights/ Const. law | -- | 1 (0.5) | 3 (2.0) | 32 (17.7) | 51 (42.9) | 116 (100)c | 203 | 1.4 | 3.4 |
| Labor | -- | 1 (0.5) | 1 (1.1) | 34 (19.8) | 57 (51.1)c | 89 (100) | 182 | 1.4 | 2.7 |
| Tax | -- | -- | -- | 12 (24.5) | 12 (49.0) | 25 (100)c | 49 | 1.2 | 2.4 |
| Bankruptcy | -- | -- | -- | 3 (15.8) | 5 (42.1) | 11 (100)c | 19 | 1.1 | 2.5 |
| Condemnation | -- | -- | -- | 3 (8.6) | 5 (22.9) | 27 (100)c | 35 | 0.5 | 2.1 |
| Seizure | -- | -- | -- | 2 (5.3) | 2 (10.5) | 34 (100)c | 38 | 0.4 | 3.8 |
| ICC | -- | -- | 1 (2.1) | 2 (6.3) | 9 (25.0) | 36 (100)c | 48 | 0.7 | 2.8 |
| Prisoner | 1 (0.2) | -- | 1 (0.5) | 7 (2.1) | 13 (5.1) | 411 (100)c | 433 | 0.2 | 4.1 |
| Admn. appeals | -- | -- | -- | 1 (1.1) | 5 (6.6) | 85 (100)c | 91 | 0.1 | 2.0 |
| Summary | 13 (0.4) | 20 (1.1) | 115 (5.1) | 685 (28.6) | 605 (49.4) | 1,471 (100) | 2,909 | 2.0 | 3.9 |

Note: The percentage of cases in each request category was cumulated from 31+ to 0.

[a]Areas of litigation are presented in descending order by average requests for all cases.

[b]This category included Jones Act cases.

[c]Category with median case.

Although every subject matter area had many cases with no discovery, the concentration of high-volume discovery cases in the top five areas is pronounced. Of the 148 cases with high-volume discovery, 120 fell into these five areas, accounting for 8 to 12 percent of the filings in each area. Conversely, the remaining ten areas had very few high-volume cases; only the contract area exceeded 2 percent. Subject matter appears to have sufficient effect on discovery use to warrant its use as a measure in any management scheme. To sharpen the predictive value, we turn to the finer categories of subject matter—case types.

All the case types in the sample were ranked according to the percentage of case filings with high-volume discovery. Every case type in which approximately 10 percent or more of the cases fell in the high-volume category was selected for analysis.[102] Statistics on the twelve case types meeting this standard are reported in table 17.[103]

In each of these case types, 9.7 percent of the case filings were in the high-volume discovery category. These case types constituted a sizeable segment of the civil docket, comprising 23.2 percent of the sampled cases.

In setting time schedules for discovery, judges should consider that any case that falls within these twelve case types is likely to involve 2.06 more discovery requests[104] than the paradigm case.[105]

## Number of Parties

All parties to a lawsuit have the right to use devices provided by the rules to obtain information and materials. It was therefore expected that

---

a suit by individual prisoners at a Maryland correctional institution, claiming damages for injuries inflicted by guards during a prison disturbance. The second case, which involved 36 discovery requests, was a class action by part of the prison population, making largely the same kind of claim for monetary damages due to injuries sustained in the disturbance, but also seeking injunctive relief against the state prison administrator to prevent any recurrence of alleged brutal conduct by guards. In chapter seven, procedures are recommended for channeling such cases along a discovery track once they have been identified as requiring discovery activity.

102. Thirty-two case types out of 108 had at least one case with high-volume discovery. For an analysis of discovery use by all case types, see appendix E.

103. "Tort-miscellaneous" requires some explanation; the category includes tort cases, such as one involving a tree falling on a car, that could not be placed in other tort categories defined by the nature of the tort or its instrumentality.

104. The F-value indicates that this increase is statistically significant at the .01 level; the presence of this factor accounted for 3.8 percent of the variance in requests for the discovered-case population.

105. See note 96 supra.

more parties in a case would mean more discovery.[106] Figure 3 depicts the relationship between the number of parties[107] and the amount of discovery.

## TABLE 17

### CASE TYPES WITH FREQUENT FILINGS
### THAT INVOLVE HIGH-VOLUME DISCOVERY

| Case Types | Total Filings | Filings with High-Volume Discovery (% of Total Filings) |
|---|---|---|
| Tort--product liability | 60 | 17 (28.3) |
| Patent | 34 | 9 (26.5) |
| Contract--franchise | 23 | 6 (26.1) |
| Contract--warranty | 25 | 4 (16.0) |
| Tort--malpractice (legal/medical) | 13 | 2 (15.4) |
| Jones Act and seaman's injury | 277 | 36 (13.0) |
| Tort--miscellaneous | 69 | 9 (13.0) |
| Tort--airline | 25 | 3 (12.0) |
| Trade regulation | 50 | 6 (12.0) |
| Securities | 87 | 10 (11.5) |
| Tort--slip and fall | 27 | 3 (11.1) |
| Contract--realty | 31 | 3 (9.7) |

---

106. The cases that contained rulings on motions to certify a class (rule 23) were also examined. It was expected that these cases might have had more discovery because of the factual issues attendant to certification of a class and because of the complexity of some recent class action cases. As evidenced by the table below, the distribution of cases by volume of discovery was not much different from that shown in table 10 for the whole discovered-case population. It should be noted, however, that the small number of cases in the table makes comparisons quite risky.

Cases with Rulings on Rule 23
Motions by Discovery Volume

| Volume Categories | No. Cases | % Cases |
|---|---|---|
| Low | 20 | 47.6 |
| Moderate | 19 | 45.2 |
| High | 3 | 7.1 |

107. In some instances, several persons listed in the style of the case had a common interest in the outcome, and counsel filed materials with the

FIGURE 3

PERCENTAGE OF CASES BY DISCOVERY
VOLUME CATEGORIES AND BY
NUMBER OF PARTIES IN DISCOVERED CASES

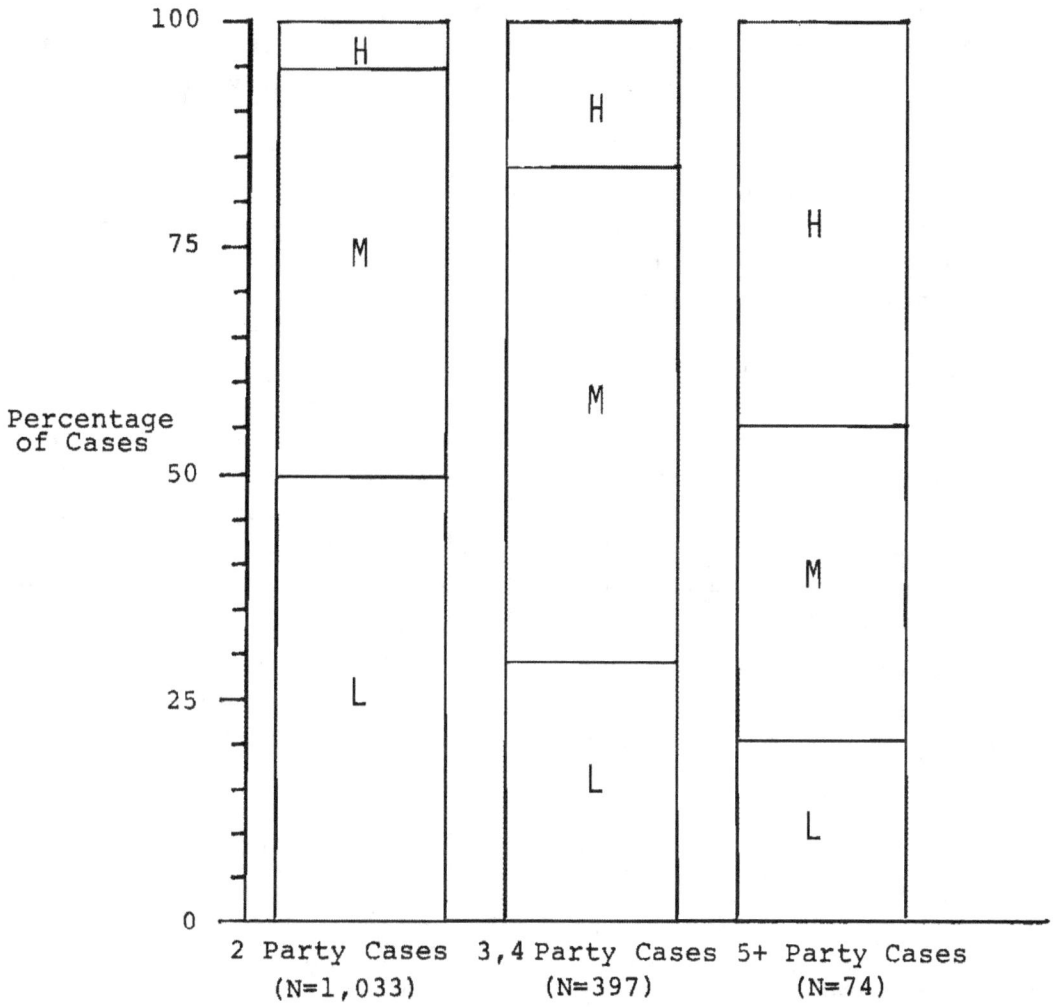

H   High-volume cases: more than 10 requests
M   Moderate-volume cases: 3-10 requests
L   Low-volume cases: 1-2 requests

The portions of high-, moderate-, and low-volume discovery in the discovered-case population are shown for cases with two, three or four, and five or more parties.

The figure shows that there is a strong positive relationship between the number of parties and the amount of discovery. Although the portion of moderate-volume cases remained fairly stable for all three categories of parties, the share of low-volume cases decreased as the number of parties increased, and high-volume cases exhibited a reciprocal pattern.

The percentage of cases with five or more parties and high-volume discovery was eight times the percentage of two-party high-volume cases, although two-party cases accounted for more than 70 percent of the discovered cases.

The judge should take into account the number of real parties in interest as a predictor of discovery use. Each addition of a real party in interest, over the basic one plaintiff and one defendant, increased the average number of discovery requests by 1.05.[108]

## Counterclaims and Cross Claims

Counterclaims and cross claims were also examined to determine their impact on discovery. Since each claim may generate some discovery by a claimant and a defendant, it was expected that the more numerous the claims and defenses, the more voluminous would be the discovery. Thus, in cases with counterclaim or cross-claim activity,[109] we would expect more requests for discovery than in cases with equal numbers of parties but without these extra claims.

### Counterclaims

To test the effects of the filing of a counterclaim on discovery, we compared the number of requests in cases with and without a counter claim.[110]

---

court on behalf of all represented parties. Using all named parties for our analysis might have distorted the effect under study. Therefore, since canon 5 of the American Bar Association's Code of Professional Responsibility forbids an attorney to represent parties with divergent interests in a case, we used the number of lawyers or law firms filing papers in a case to determine "commonality of interest" and to identify the number of plaintiffs, defendants, third-party defendants, and intervenors.

108. The F-value indicates that this increase is statistically significant at the .01 level; the presence of this factor accounted for 8.2 percent of the variance in requests for the discovered-case population.

109. Rule 13(a) requires the filing of counterclaims in some cases and permits them in others. Rule 13(g) permits a party to assert against a co-party a cross claim arising out of the transaction or occurrence that is the subject matter of the original claim.

110. The group of cases without a counterclaim had the following charac-

Figure 4 shows that a positive correlation exists between the presence of a controverted counterclaim and the number of discovery requests. Indeed, cases with a counterclaim had nearly twice as many discovery requests as cases with only a complaint and answer. It appears that each party generates about the same number of discovery requests when the only claim is in the original complaint. The addition of a counterclaim by the defendant increases total discovery, which remains equally divided between the parties.

Again, the filing of counterclaims in a case appears to be a reliable predictor of additional discovery. Cases with one or more counterclaims averaged 2.2 more requests than cases without any extra claims.[111]

Cross Claims

To test the effects of cross claims on discovery, cases with and without these claims were compared in largely the same way as in the counterclaim analysis.[112]

Figure 5 shows that controverted cross claims added an average of 2.8 discovery requests to a case.[113] Although substantial, the increase in discovery produced by controverted cross claims was not as great as that produced by controverted counterclaims. In contrast to the discovery increase from counterclaims, however, the cross-claim increase was entirely accounted for by defendants.

Amount in Controversy

It was suspected that the damages claimed could influence the amount of discovery, due to the financial incentives or disincentives resulting from the expected recovery.[114]

---

teristics: one plaintiff and one defendant, a complaint and answer, and a discovery request. The group with a counterclaim had all the other group's characteristics and had a counterclaim and counterclaim answer filed.

111. The F-value indicates that this increase is statistically significant at the .01 level; the presence of this factor accounted for 1.8 percent of the variance in requests for the discovered-case population.

112. The two populations that were compared had the following characteristic events: The group of cases without cross claims had two original complaints (one plaintiff and two defendants), two answers to the complaint, and a discovery request. The group with cross claims had the same events as the other group, but also had at least one cross claim and at least one cross-claim answer.

113. The F-value indicates that this increase is statistically significant at the .01 level; the presence of this factor accounted for 1 percent of the variance in requests for the discovered-case population.

114. In each of the sampled cases, the amount claimed by the plaintiff was recorded. No effort was made to record amendments to the pleadings increasing the ad damnum clause, amounts sought by defendants in either counterclaims or cross claims, or amounts sought by intervenors.

# FIGURE 4

## COMPARISON OF AVERAGE DISCOVERY REQUESTS
## BETWEEN CASES WITH AND WITHOUT
## CONTROVERTED COUNTERCLAIM

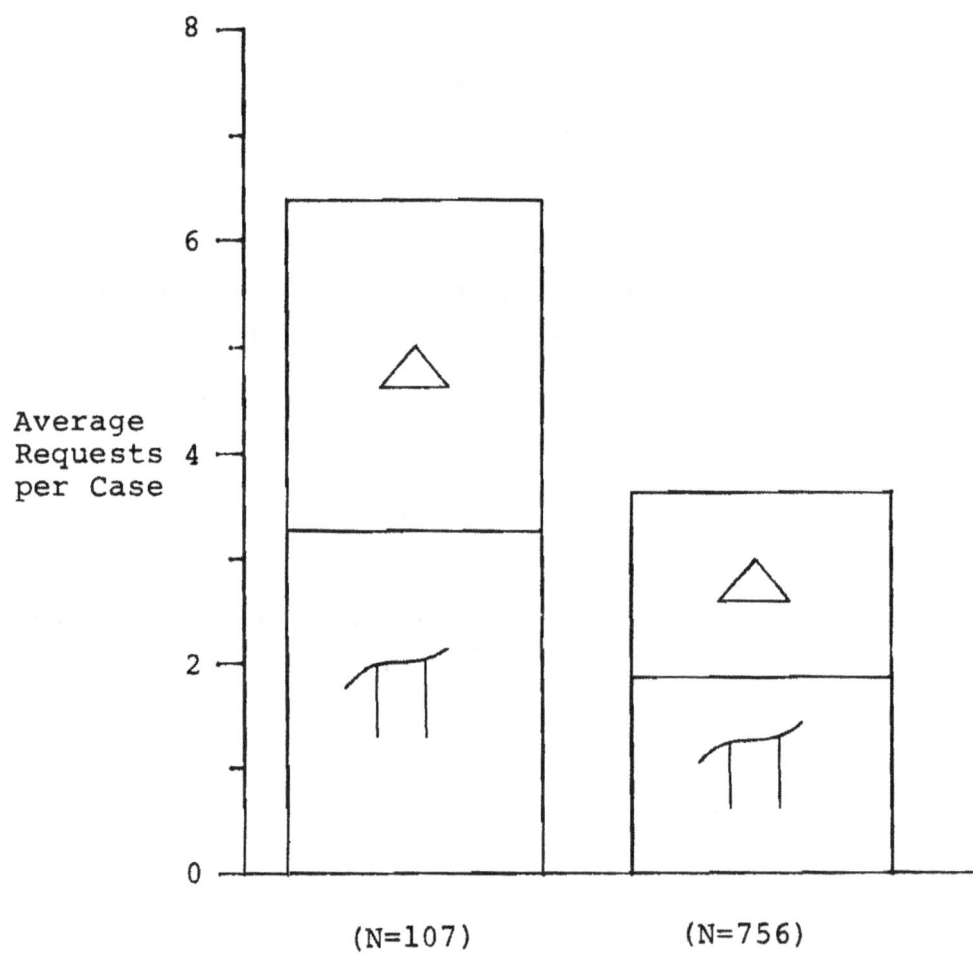

FIGURE 5

COMPARISON OF AVERAGE DISCOVERY REQUESTS
BETWEEN CASES WITH AND WITHOUT
CONTROVERTED CROSS CLAIM

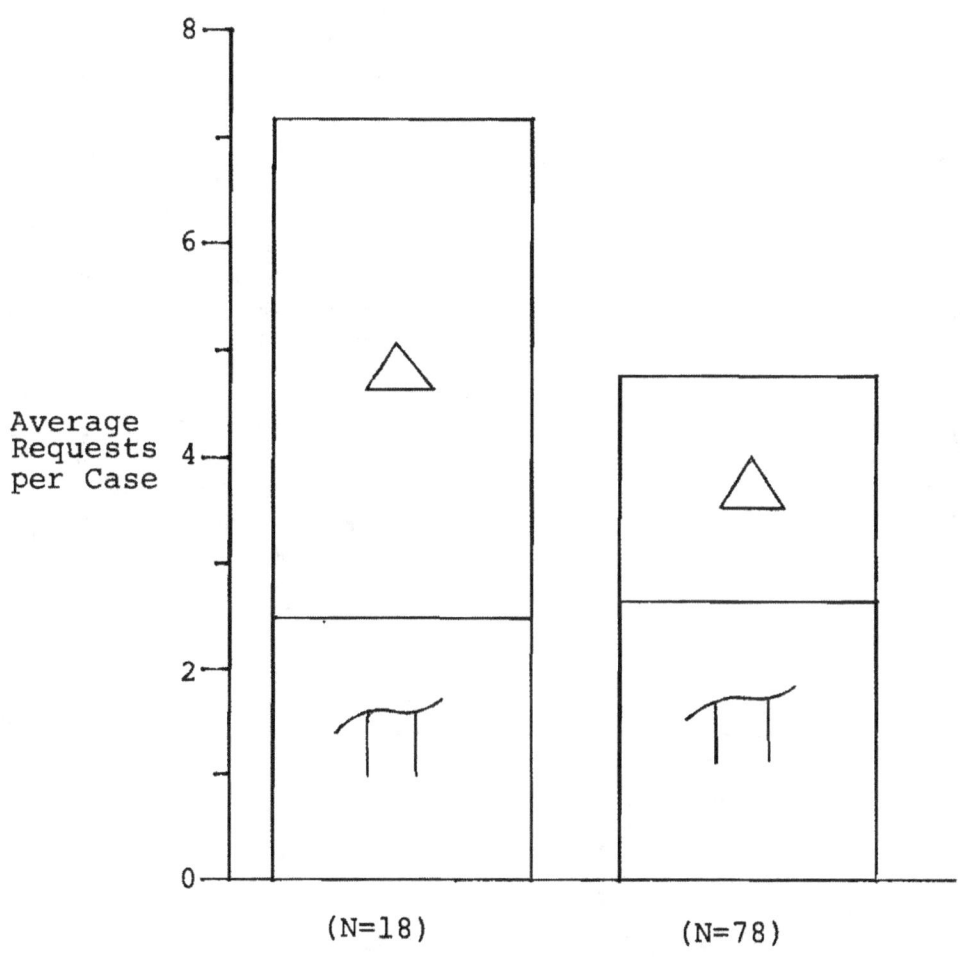

Average
Requests
per Case

(N=18)

(N=78)

With Cross Claim    Without Cross Claim

△    Average requests by defendant
π    Average requests by plaintiff

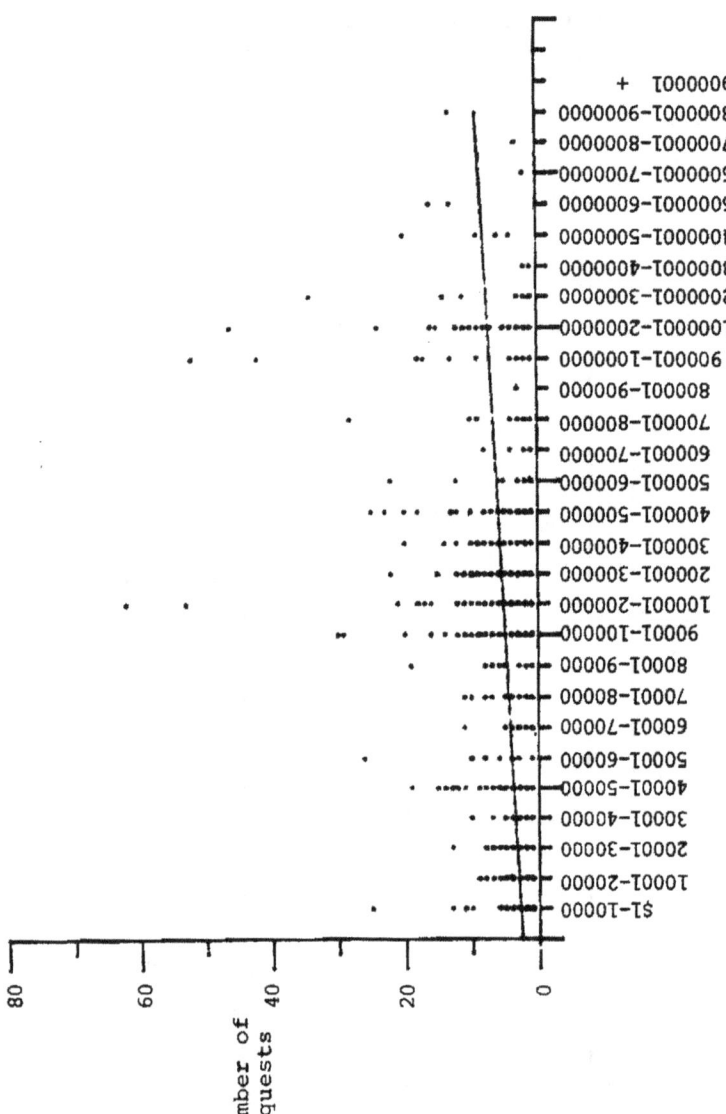

FIGURE 6

RELATIONSHIP BETWEEN AMOUNT IN CONTROVERSY AND
NUMBER OF DISCOVERY REQUESTS

Dollar Amount in Controversy Grouped

Note: The point plot and the least squares regression line were both
calculated after the grouping transformation was performed.

Figure 6 shows the relationship between the amount in controversy and the number of discovery requests.[115] The fact that the regression line is sloped indicates that there is a correlation between the two variables, but the slightness of the slope shows that differences in amounts in controversy did not account for much of the difference in amounts of discovery.[116]

Using $100,000 as a line of demarcation, cases claiming more than that amount averaged 1.2 more discovery requests than those with less. Although the increase was statistically significant,[117] the slightness of the difference makes the amount in controversy a less reliable predictor of increased discovery than other characteristics studied. Apparently, the amount claimed by the plaintiff in the complaint bears little relationship to the actual value of the case. In considering characteristics of the pleadings, however, judges should be alert to the possibility that very large monetary claims could involve increased discovery.

In sum, data in this chapter have shown that a regular system of managing discovery can be implemented based on early signals of increased discovery activity. The pleadings help in selecting a management track for a case and in selecting an appropriate cutoff date for discovery. This should save the judicial resources needed to administer the case management system, by reducing the number of motions seeking postponements of cutoff dates. Chapters five and six will show that the imposition of discovery timing controls produces significant time savings in discovery and in the total time required to terminate civil cases.

---

115. Cases were studied if the plaintiff claimed money damages and at least one request for discovery was filed.

116. The filing practices of pro se plaintiffs did not appear to have an impact on this relationship. Only 7 of the 202 cases in which a plaintiff proceeded pro se had monetary claims for recovery, and the median amount in those cases was only $2,500.

117. The F-value indicates statistical significance at the .01 level; the presence of this factor accounted for 0.8 percent of the variance in requests for the discovered-case population.

CHAPTER V

## THE IMPACT OF JUDICIAL CONTROLS ON DISCOVERY

Federal judges use a variety of methods to control discovery.[118] Discovery timing controls, particularly cutoff dates, were employed by some courts and some judges in the sampled cases. Variations in practice offered an opportunity to compare results. Judges who seek to regain control of discovery through cutoff dates expect elapsed discovery time to be shortened. Data presented in this chapter show that the expectation can be fulfilled.

No matter how effective discovery timing controls might be, they would be unacceptable if they seriously constrained the exercise of discovery rights. Accordingly, we also examined whether discovery timing controls (1) resulted in less discovery or (2) altered the pattern of discovery requests.

The answer to both inquiries was negative. We conclude that discovery timing controls result in closer conformity to rule provisions specifying time limits for responses to requests, and reduce the time between requests (initiation time), a matter not governed by any federal rule. The time savings are not achieved at the cost of observable interference with quantity or choice of discovery requests.

Data adduced in this chapter demonstrate that discovery timing controls under rule 83 fill the control vacuum created by the gradual relaxation of rule control discussed in chapter one.

## Effects of Judge Control on Overall Discovery Times

Categories and definitions set the stage for analysis. Judges in the six courts were classified based on their use of discovery cutoff dates. The following four criteria determined the classification:

1.  Consistency. Discovery cutoff dates were set in almost all civil cases.

2.  Earliness. Discovery cutoff dates were set approximately ninety days after the date of issue.

3.  Shortness. A period of about 120 days or less was usually allowed for discovery activity.

---

118. See generally T. Guyer, Survey of Local Civil Discovery Procedures (Federal Judicial Center 1977).

4. <u>Firmness</u>. Requests for enlargements of the discovery periods were infrequently granted.

Judges who met all four criteria were placed in the "strong control" group; other judges were placed in the "limited or no control" group.[119] The latter group was very heterogeneous, including judges who imposed no controls as well as judges whose practices met some but not all of the four control criteria.

A two-step process, using both "hard" and "soft" data, was employed to place the judges into one of the two groups. The initial classification was based on data obtained in each court from observations and interviews conducted during phase one of the District Court Studies Project.[120] These classifications were then verified from the statistical data.[121] The initial classifications were confirmed, except for six judges who were moved from one category to another.

Composition of the groups is shown in table 18. The fifty-four judges

TABLE 18

CLASSIFICATION OF JUDGES BY DISCOVERY
CONTROL GROUP AND BY COURT
(Number of Judges)

| Court | Judges Using Strong Controls | Judges Using Limited or No Controls | Total |
|-------|------------------------------|-------------------------------------|-------|
| S.Fla. | 7 | 0 | 7 |
| C.Cal. | 9 | 5 | 14 |
| Md. | 2 | 3 | 5 |
| E.La. | 2 | 5 | 7 |
| E.Pa. | 6 | 10 | 16 |
| Mass. | 0 | 5 | 5 |
| All courts | 26 | 28 | 54 |

---

119. Requiring all four criteria makes this test quite conservative. This high standard was used because, as is more fully explained in chapter seven, all four criteria are required in order to derive maximum benefit from discovery controls. A less conservative classification, comparing judges who met all four criteria with judges who met none, would likely show even more substantial differences than those reported herein.

Nine judges could not be classified, and their cases were not included in any of the statistics measuring the effects of judge control: two in Central California, two in Maryland, two in Eastern Louisiana, two in Eastern Pennsylvania, and one in Massachusetts. Either they were too close to the borderline or there was too little information. Also, some of these judges had changed procedures during the time period under study.

120. For a description of the methodology used in phase one, see Case Management report, <u>supra</u> note 7, at 1-6, 79-83.

121. Statistical data on the judges alone could not be relied on, because

were almost evenly divided between the two groups, but the two groups were not evenly represented among courts:  Southern Florida had no judges in the limited-or-no-control group, and Massachusetts had none in the strong-control group.

Time measures must also be defined.  To ascertain the overall impact of control on the time needed to complete discovery, we measured "total discovery time," that is, the elapsed time from the first discovery request to the last recorded discovery event,[122] whether that event was a request, a response,[123] or an event in the discovery motion process.

Average total discovery times are presented in table 19.  Cases before judges who used strong controls exhibited dramatically shorter discovery times than cases before judges who used limited or no controls.  For judges using strong controls, total discovery time averaged more than eight months less in completed cases and about five months less in discovered cases.

### TABLE 19

#### TOTAL DISCOVERY TIMES BY JUDGE-CONTROL GROUPS
(Average Days)

| Case Population | Judges Using Strong Controls | Judges Using Limited or No Controls |
|---|---|---|
| Discovered cases (N=1,158) | 176 | 334 |
| Completed cases (N=343) | 253 | 505 |

The data were subjected to statistical analysis (t-test) to determine whether the observed differences might have been the result of chance.  Based on the results,[124] we exclude that possibility and conclude that

---

in the courts with large numbers of judgeships (Eastern Pennsylvania and Central California), there were too few sampled cases per judge to make reliable classifications.

122.  Cases that had only one discovery event would produce no duration and were therefore excluded from this calculation.  An example would be a case in which a set of interrogatories was filed but the case was terminated before a response or any other discovery event was recorded.

123.  We need to elaborate on the instances in which a response was the "last discovery event" in calculating total discovery time.  That event would be either the filing of a response to a request, or the deposition notice, or the holding of a deposition as evidenced by the transcript filed with the court.  The attorney interviews indicated, however, that although attorneys usually file answers or objections to requests, they don't file transcripts of depositions nearly as frequently.  See appendix C.  Therefore, in cases in which the last discovery event was a deposition without a filed transcript, we used the date for which the deposition was noticed.

124.  The t-values, 9.07 (discovered cases) and 6.94 (completed cases),

the observed differences are associated with the factors that defined the two groups--the use of discovery timing controls.

Table 20 displays time differences for the two control groups, broken down by discovery volume categories. We sought here to determine whether the accelerated pace resulting from control was achieved consistently across the categories. The table provides six comparisons; in every instance, discovery in cases before the strong-control group was accomplished in substantially less time than that required in cases before the limited-or-no-control group. Acceleration occurs regardless of the amount of discovery sought by the parties.[125]

TABLE 20

TOTAL DISCOVERY TIMES BY JUDGE-CONTROL GROUPS
AND BY VOLUME CATEGORIES
(Average Days)

| Volume Categories | Total Discovery Time in Discovered Cases | | Total Discovery Time in Completed Cases | |
| --- | --- | --- | --- | --- |
| | Judges Using Strong Controls | Judges Using Limited or No Controls | Judges Using Strong Controls | Judges Using Limited or No Controls |
| Low | 65 | 135 | 87 | 179 |
| Moderate | 166 | 387 | 200 | 504 |
| High | 450 | 863 | 475 | 894 |

#### Effects of Court Control on Overall Discovery Times

Establishing that there are systematic differences in the duration of discovery activity before judges who do and do not employ strong controls over discovery is but the first step in the analysis of the effects of control. The next issue is the extent to which the prevailing practice of a court regarding discovery timing controls affects the duration of discovery. Two questions will be addressed in this section: (1) Does the prevailing court practice affect total discovery time for the district? and (2) Does the prevailing court practice affect the results obtained by individual judges using similar discovery timing controls?

Answering these questions requires classifying the courts by their degree of control, using a process similar to that used to classify the judges. An initial classification drew on the interviews and observations

---

were both significant at the .001 level.

125. The main effects for both judge control and volume category in both populations were significant at the .001 level. The two-way interaction was also significant in both populations, at the .001 level for discovered cases and at the .01 level for completed cases.

in phase one of the project concerning attempts by the courts, as a whole, to monitor and control discovery time. A court was considered to have complete control if it was observed to have subjected the bulk of its civil docket to the four criteria of discovery timing control used to classify judges. Only Southern Florida and Central California met this test; the remaining courts were ranked according to the nature and extent of other forms of control used, such as monitoring the civil docket by regularly holding status conferences. As with the classification of the judges, statistical data were used to verify the observations of the researchers.

On the basis of all information available, the six courts were ranked from most to least controlling as follows: (1) Southern Florida, (2) Central California, (3) Maryland, (4) Eastern Louisiana, (5) Eastern Pennsylvania, (6) Massachusetts. The following paragraphs will provide some detail about the judicial discovery control procedures in the courts studied.[126]

### Southern District of Florida

The Southern District of Florida exercised the strictest control over discovery of all the courts studied. In most civil cases, within a few days after the last answer to the complaint was filed, a notice was sent to the attorneys setting both a cutoff date for discovery and a final pretrial conference.[127] The time permitted for discovery was based on the complexity of the case as revealed by pleadings. If the parties later demonstrated that diligent discovery had been under way but that additional time was needed, the judges postponed the cutoff date to a specific time.

### Central District of California

Pursuant to local rule 9, nearly every case was subjected to a sixty-day discovery cutoff date shortly after joinder of issue. Central California judges, however, were more liberal in granting postponements than were Southern Florida judges. In fact, interviews with court personnel indicated that from one to three postponements of the cutoff date were routinely granted.

### District of Maryland

Maryland had no local rule providing for discovery timing controls. Only two judges regularly set and enforced discovery cutoff dates, but most of the civil docket was subject to controls. However, control in some of

---

126. In classifying the courts, the discovery controls--or other forms of control--exerted over prisoner, administrative appeals, and seizure cases were not considered.

127. Local rule 14(f) requires that all discovery be completed five days before the final pretrial conference unless leave of court is granted.

those cases was limited: One judge generally gave the parties substantially more time to discover than did the judges in either Southern Florida or Central California, and another judge in the same group did not always enforce the cutoff dates. Two other judges depended on status conferences to control discovery.

### Eastern District of Louisiana

Status conferences were the prime form of discovery control in the Eastern District of Louisiana. Some judges did set cutoff dates for discovery, but less than half of the civil docket was controlled in this way. When cutoff dates were set, estimates of counsel rather than independent judgment of the court were used to determine the discovery time allowed.

### Eastern District of Pennsylvania

In the Eastern District of Pennsylvania, twelve judges exercised limited or no control over discovery timing. The other six judges generally set cutoff dates, and about one-third of the civil docket was subject to these controls. Often, however, controls were imposed by the court sometime after discovery had begun. Many of the cutoff dates were not firmly enforced.

### District of Massachusetts

Of the six district judges in Massachusetts, only one made a systematic attempt to control discovery time, but he usually did not enforce the cutoff dates set. Most of the other judges used periodic status conferences to monitor discovery activity.

For analysis purposes, the six courts were divided into three categories. Southern Florida and Central California are the strongest and most systematic controllers of discovery (hereafter most-controlling courts); Eastern Pennsylvania and Massachusetts have the least control (hereafter least-controlling courts); and Maryland and Eastern Louisiana fall between these extremes (moderate-controlling courts).

The effects of court-wide control on total discovery time in discovered and completed cases are displayed in table 21.

As shown in table 21, the control exerted by a court had a substantial effect on discovery time. Stronger control produced shorter average total discovery times.[128] Differences between court categories in durations of discovery were large. For example, in completed cases, the parties in the most-controlling courts filed their last discovery event an average of 338 days earlier than the parties in the least-controlling courts.

---

128. The F-values--for discovered cases, 38.91, and for completed cases, 34.62--were both significant at the .001 level.

TABLE 21

TOTAL DISCOVERY TIMES BY CATEGORY OF COURT CONTROL
(Average Days)

| Case Population | Most-Controlling Courts | Moderate-Controlling Courts | Least-Controlling Courts |
|---|---|---|---|
| Discovered cases (N=1,334) | 185 | 249 | 347 |
| Completed cases (N=394) | 270 | 321 | 608 |

## Effects of Combined Judge and Court Control on Overall Discovery Times

Further analysis was undertaken to determine whether individual judge controls were affected by the prevailing control environment of the court in which the judge worked. Because the local bar may respond to the procedures established by the majority of judges, it was thought that judges using strong controls in the most-controlling courts were likely to achieve shorter discovery times than judges using strong controls in less-controlling courts. Table 22 presents data on the combined effects of judge and court control. The columns show the average total discovery time for each of the three court-control categories and the rows show that average for the two judge-control groups within each court category. Both the discovered- and completed-case populations are shown.

TABLE 22

TOTAL DISCOVERY TIMES BY EXTENT
OF JUDGE AND COURT CONTROL
(Average Days)

| Case Populations | Most-Controlling Courts | Moderate-Controlling Courts | Least-Controlling Courts |
|---|---|---|---|
| Discovered cases before: Judges using strong controls | 163 | 179 | 223 |
| Judges using limited or no controls | 271 | 286 | 382 |
| Completed cases before: Judges using strong controls | 255 | 222 | 343 |
| Judges using limited or no controls | 381 | 377 | 661 |

Table 22 provides twelve observations of the combined effect of judge control and court control. Ten of the twelve display the anticipated effect: Judges using strong controls achieved prompter discovery when working in most-controlling courts, and less promptness as the strength of court control declined.[129] Judges using limited controls experienced greater promptness working in most-controlling courts and the least promptness when working in least-controlling courts. The only departures from the anticipated pattern occurred when, in the completed-case population, judges in both judge-control groups in the moderate-controlling courts produced shorter durations than their counterparts in the most-controlling courts.

We conclude therefore that reduction in the time required for making discovery is affected by overall court practice in using timing controls and by individual judge practice. We further conclude that the potential effects that any individual judge can expect from discovery timing controls are affected by the court environment. Doubtless there will be occasional exceptions, but the data presented here make a strong case that the very best efforts of a judge using strong controls will meet with smaller rewards in a less-controlling court than will similar efforts in a more-controlling court.

### Control and Patterns of Requesting Discovery

Control has been demonstrated to shorten total discovery time. The next question is whether control affects the way in which parties use discovery.

Do strong controls achieve shorter total discovery time by discouraging the exercise of discovery rights? It was possible that attorneys, faced with an approaching cutoff date for discovery, might sacrifice fully discovering a case in order to meet the deadline. This issue was examined by computing the average requests per discovery case for judge, court, and combined judge- and court-control categories. If attorneys do sacrifice their discovery rights because of control, the number of requests per case should decrease as control increases.

Table 23 reports the average recorded requests per case for all combinations of control variables. These data indicate that imposition of controls does not reduce litigating attorneys' discovery activity. Indeed, based on recorded activity, the opposite result was observed. Cases before judges using strong controls in the most-controlling courts had more requests than cases before judges using limited controls in the least-controlling courts.[130]

---

129. For both the discovered- and completed-case populations, the main effects for both judge control and court control are significant at the .001 level. The interaction is not significant.

130. An analysis of variance indicated that there was a significant main effect for court control (p = less than .05). There was no significant main effect found for judge control, nor was there a significant interaction effect.

TABLE 23

AVERAGE REQUESTS PER DISCOVERED CASE
BY EXTENT OF JUDGE AND COURT CONTROL

|  | Cases in Most-Controlling Courts | Cases in Moderate-Controlling Courts | Cases in Least-Controlling Courts | Cases in All Courts |
|---|---|---|---|---|
| Cases before judges using strong controls | 5.48 | 4.02 | 5.16 | 5.17 |
| Cases before judges using limited or no controls | 3.86 | 3.95 | 4.74 | 4.34 |
| Cases before all judges | 5.19 | 3.97 | 4.83 | 4.72 |

Though intuition leads to an expectation of reduced discovery in response to strong control, we had anticipated that attorneys in strong-control situations might file (rather than not file) their discovery requests to lay the groundwork for postponing the cutoff date. The information obtained in the survey of filing practices[131] confirmed that expectation. Other factors, such as local state practice and the existence of a highly specialized bar in some areas of practice, also affected the frequency of filing.

When formal (recorded) discovery activity is adjusted to take informal (unrecorded) activity into account, no systematic pattern of increase in response to discovery controls can be discerned. Southern Florida and Central California, the most-controlling courts, ranked fourth and first, respectively, in average requests per case. Eastern Pennsylvania and Massachusetts, the least-controlling courts, ranked second and sixth. Moreover, the statistical analysis makes it impossible to reject the null hypothesis; i.e., that control has no effect on the extent of discovery activity.

We have shown that control does not affect the quantity of discovery activity. Does control alter discovery patterns in a qualitative way that impairs effective use of discovery rights? Two possibilities were considered. Attorneys before judges using strong controls might feel constrained to cluster their requests rather than distribute them evenly over the discovery time period. We do not refer here to the sequence of filing a request, waiting for a response, filing another request, waiting for a response, and so on until all discovery is completed. We refer only to the

---

131. Survey results are fully reported in appendix C.

spacing of requests during the time actually used for discovery. For example, if the total amount of time between the first and the last discovery request was 100 days, and there were eleven requests, completely unclustered requests would come at 10-day intervals over the 100 days; completely clustered requests would all be filed on the same day.

Without considering any hypothetical standard of maximum effectiveness, we sought only to determine whether there was a substantial difference in the patterns of discovery in strong- and limited-control situations. Table 24 presents the results, on a scale of zero to one; zero represents completely unclustered requests, and one represents completely clustered ones.

TABLE 24

EXTENT OF CLUSTERING REQUESTS BY JUDGE-CONTROL
AND COURT-CONTROL GROUPS
(Average Clustering Factor)

| Judges Using Strong Controls | | Judges Using Limited or No Controls |
|---|---|---|
| .66 | | .64 |
| Most-Controlling Courts | Moderate-Controlling Courts | Least-Controlling Courts |
| .66 | .63 | .65 |

Legend:  0 = minimum clustering
         1 = maximum clustering

Note:  Cases with three or more requests by plaintiffs or defendants were studied. None of the differences were statistically significant.

There is no measurable difference between the patterns of discovery in the two judge-control and three court-control groups. It is interesting to note that all the values, regardless of control, exceed .50, indicating that substantial clustering is the prevailing pattern.

Since attorneys tend to cluster discovery requests independently of the control variable, we also questioned whether control might result in a greater imbalance of discovery requests (whether clustered or unclustered) at one end or the other of the litigation process. Again, we report our findings using a scale of zero to one; zero means that all requests were filed at the very beginning of the discovery request period, and one means that all requests were filed at the very end. The results for the two judge-control groups and the three court-control groups are presented in table 25. The data indicate that the balance in timing of discovery requests, relative to the entire time used for requests, is not affected by the imposition of controls.

TABLE 25

TIMING BALANCE IN DISCOVERY REQUESTS
BY JUDGE-CONTROL AND COURT-CONTROL GROUPS
(Average Balance Factor per Discovered Case)

| Judges Using Strong Controls | | Judges Using Limited or No Controls |
|---|---|---|
| .46 | | .50 |

| Most-Controlling Courts | Moderate-Controlling Courts | Least-Controlling Courts |
|---|---|---|
| .46 | .54 | .46 |

Note:  Cases with three or more requests by plaintiffs or defendants were studied.  None of the differences were statistically significant.

## Response and Initiation Time

We have seen that discovery timing controls produce shorter total discovery time.  We now seek to determine where in the discovery process the time saving is achieved.  Two significant intervals were examined:  (1) the time from request to response (response time) and (2) the time between individual requests (initiation time).

### Response Time

Tables 26 and 27 show the effect of control on response time, by judge- and court-control categories, for the four types of discovery requests most frequently used by attorneys.  Table 26 reports the durations for the two judge groups, and table 27 for the three court groups.

Controlling courts and judges using strong controls achieved the greatest impact on response times to interrogatories and document requests. Responses to interrogatories in cases before judges who used strong controls were filed about one-and-a-half months earlier than responses in cases before judges using limited controls.  Responses to document requests were filed about one month earlier.  Comparison of response times in cases before the most-controlling and least-controlling courts exhibited similar relationships.  Deposition times were also substantially shortened.

Requests for admissions provided the only exception to an otherwise consistent pattern of reduced response time in cases subjected to stronger discovery controls.  The slightly shorter time for this request type in cases before judges who used strong controls was not statistically signifi-

TABLE 26

RESPONSE DURATIONS BY JUDGE-CONTROL GROUPS
FOR SELECTED REQUEST TYPES
(Average Days)

|  | Interrogatory (N=1,484) | Oral Deposition[a] (N=762) | Document Request (N=281) | Admissions Request[b] (N=229) |
|---|---|---|---|---|
| Strong-control group | 72 | 23 | 44 | 43 |
| Limited-or-no-control group | 117 | 33 | 76 | 48 |

[a]This measures the duration from the first notice of a deposition to the date of the holding of the deposition.

[b]The difference in the admissions request category was not statistically significant. All other differences were significant at the .001 level.

TABLE 27

RESPONSE DURATIONS BY COURT-CONTROL GROUPS
FOR SELECTED REQUEST TYPES
(Average Days)

|  | Interrogatory (N=1,715) | Oral Deposition[a] (N=883) | Document Request (N=310) | Admissions Request[b] (N=251) |
|---|---|---|---|---|
| Most-controlling courts | 64 | 20 | 42 | 47 |
| Moderate-controlling courts | 91 | 29 | 64 | 49 |
| Least-controlling courts | 124 | 46 | 80 | 40 |

[a]This measures the duration from the first notice of a deposition to the date of the holding of the deposition.

[b]The difference in the admissions request category was not statistically significant. All other differences were significant at the .001 level.

cant. Comparison of response times to requests for admissions in the three court-control categories shows no relationship between control and time. This is probably accounted for by the virtually automatic sanction of having the matter admitted unless denied or objected to within thirty days--an incentive that operates independently of discovery control practice.

Are shorter response times achieved simply because responding attorneys before judges who use strong controls file responses faster, or is the result achieved at least partly because requesting attorneys in strong-control situations invoke the provisions of rule 37 more frequently? To address that question, we examined the frequency of compelling motions addressed to eligible interrogatories in completed cases; i.e., interrogatories to which no answer had been filed within thirty days. Table 28 displays these data.

TABLE 28

COMPELLING MOTIONS PER ELIGIBLE INTERROGATORY
IN COMPLETED CASES BY JUDGE-CONTROL GROUPS

| Judge-Control Group | Eligible Interrogatories[a] | Compelling Motions | % of Eligible Interrogatories with Compelling Motions |
|---|---|---|---|
| Strong-control group | 56 | 21 | 37.5 |
| Limited-or-no-control group | 72 | 29 | 40.3 |

Note: An interrogatory was eligible if it had no answer filed or if the answer was filed beyond the 30-day limit.

Judges who used strong controls did not experience a greater incidence of compelling motions; in fact, the contrary is true. Cases before judges using strong controls included fewer eligible interrogatories and a smaller percentage of eligible interrogatories resulting in motions. Therefore, we conclude that strong controls produce the observed reduction in response time without increasing the judges' burden in considering compelling motions.

When compelling motions were invoked, reaction time[132] of requesting parties was also shorter for judges who used strong controls. Average reaction time to compelling motions on interrogatories was 71 days for judges using strong controls and 119 days for judges using limited controls.

Initiation Time

A savings in response time does not completely account for the observed reduction in total discovery time. Control also sharply reduces the amount of time between requests for discovery. This time savings is sub-

---

132. Reaction time is the elapsed time from the date an answer to an interrogatory first fell due to the date of filing a compelling motion.

stantial and applies to all types of requests. Neither the rules nor the judges direct lawyers when to file requests, but it was anticipated that lawyers operating under discovery timing controls would respond by initiating requests while responses were pending and while opposing counsel were initiating their discovery requests. Acceleration was expected to be related to the extent of discovery controls. The data shown in tables 29 and 30 confirmed that expectation.

TABLE 29

INITIATION TIMES BY EXTENT OF JUDGE CONTROL
(Average Days)

| Judges Using Strong Controls (N=476) | Judges Using Limited or No Controls (N=597) |
|:---:|:---:|
| 36 | 98 |

Note: Cases with two or more requests filed by plaintiffs, defendants, or third-party defendants were studied.

Table 30 presents data on average initiation time per case for cases in the three discovery volume categories and each court-control category.

TABLE 30

INITIATION TIME BY DISCOVERY VOLUME
AND BY COURT-CONTROL GROUPS
(Average Days)

| | Most-Controlling Courts (N=394) | Moderate-Controlling Courts (N=349) | Least-Controlling Courts (N=435) |
|---|:---:|:---:|:---:|
| Low (1-2 requests) | 35 | 92 | 111 |
| Moderate (3-10 requests) | 41 | 77 | 94 |
| High (11+ requests) | 23 | 51 | 54 |
| Summary | 37 | 79 | 93 |

Tables 29 and 30 show that control produces substantially shorter initiation times for discovery requests. The average initiation times in cases before judges who used strong controls were almost three times shorter than those in cases before the limited-or-no-control group.[133] There was also a strong correlation between initiation time and the degree of court control:[134] the average initiation time for the most-controlling courts was about two-and-a-half times less than that for the least-controlling courts.

The tables also show that the most substantial impact of court control was on the low-volume cases. The difference in initiation times between the most- and least-controlling courts was about thirty-one days in the high-volume cases and about seventy-six days in the low-volume cases. Since low-volume cases outnumber high-volume cases by about four to one, the savings in initiation time for the low-volume category surely contributed in a very substantial way to the shortening of total discovery time noted earlier in tables 19, 20, and 21.

Cutoff dates appear to speed discovery in two ways: the attorneys respond to requests more promptly, and they file their second, third, and subsequent requests at shorter intervals without waiting for responses to earlier requests.

In sum, the use of rule 83 to impose discovery timing controls appears to have the effect of speeding both requests and responses. The result is more rapid completion of all discovery without any perceptible increases in motion activity. As a consequence, many of the gaps of inactivity in discovery that appear when judges do not set controls are eliminated without increasing the investment of judge time.

Moreover, the use of discovery timing controls does not mean that attorneys will be impeded in fully discovering their cases. Notwithstanding the imposition of cutoff dates, attorneys still decide the formality and frequency as well as the sequence and timing of requests within the discovery period. Also, the data in this section indicate that the use of discovery timing controls does not affect the patterns of filing discovery in any measurable way and that attorneys do not file less discovery in a case that is subject to discovery controls. We shall see in the next chapter that shortened discovery time means earlier disposition of cases.

133. The differences were statistically significant. The t-value of 9.37 has a probability of less than .01.

134. An analysis of variance yielded F-values that indicated significant main effects for both level of court control (p = less than .001) and volume of discovery (p = less than .01). The interaction effects were not significant.

CHAPTER VI

## THE IMPACT OF DISCOVERY CONTROLS
## ON CASE DISPOSITION TIME

Data in the preceding chapters have shown relationships between judicial controls and elapsed time for discovery. A broader and possibly more important question is whether total case disposition time--the elapsed time from filing to termination of a case--is also reduced when discovery time is shortened.

At this point, inferences must be made cautiously, since our data on the degree of control cover only the discovery stage of a case. We will need to know the extent to which this stage is independent of other stages. We will also need to determine whether judicial controls imposed on the discovery process are part of a consistent application of controls to all stages in a case.

Dividing each case into four stages allows us to answer the questions posed above and also to determine whether, for example, changes in discovery time in turn change the amount of time required for other stages in a case. The four stages are

1. _Pleadings_: the time between the original complaint and the last event in the pleadings

2. _Discovery_: the time between the first discovery event and the last discovery event

3. _Pretrial_: the time between the last discovery event and either the beginning of the trial or the termination of the case, if it is disposed of other than by trial[135]

4. _Trial_: the number of trial days.

We will have more to say about the length of time for each stage and the degree to which there may be overlap between stages. First, we examine

---

135. "Pretrial" is not normally conceived of as a stage separate from discovery. Data from this study, however, have indicated that in cases going to trial, settlement conferences and final pretrial conferences are usually held during the often lengthy period between the completion of discovery and the date of trial. Because pretrial can be identified as a distinct time period and because of its easily identifiable characteristic events, it has been possible to treat it separately for analytical purposes. It is thus treated as a separate stage even when a trial is not held.

the relationship between the extent of judicial control over discovery time and total disposition time.

Tables 31 and 32 reveal the same pattern we observed for discovery time.[136] Both settled and tried cases were affected by controls.[137] The magnitude of the differences between the groups is striking. Settled cases before judges using strong controls had an average disposition time of 316 fewer days than those before judges using limited or no controls; for tried cases, disposition took 473 days less when strong controls were used. Indeed, tried cases before judges who used strong controls were disposed of on the average 210 days earlier (682 minus 472 in table 31) than settled cases before judges who used limited or no controls.[138]

In table 32, differences in total disposition time between the most-controlling courts and the least-controlling courts are even more striking.

TABLE 31

TOTAL DISPOSITION TIME BY EXTENT OF
JUDGE CONTROL AND BY DISPOSITION TYPE
(Average Days)

| Disposition Type | Judges Using Strong Controls | Judges Using Limited or No Controls |
| --- | --- | --- |
| Settled | 366 | 682 |
| Tried | 472 | 945 |

TABLE 32

TOTAL DISPOSITION TIME BY EXTENT OF
COURT CONTROL AND BY DISPOSITION TYPE
(Average Days)

| Disposition Type | Most-Controlling Courts | Moderate-Controlling Courts | Least-Controlling Courts |
| --- | --- | --- | --- |
| Settled | 385 | 523 | 695 |
| Tried | 467 | 667 | 1,117 |

136. A case was included if a filed discovery request produced a response. The case populations studied in tables 31 through 35 were the same as those used to display discovery time in tables 19 through 22, supra.

137. This analysis of total disposition time omits from consideration cases terminated by voluntary dismissal and motions. Plaintiffs usually voluntarily dismiss a claim before commencing discovery; therefore, most of these cases are unaffected by discovery timing controls. Although some cases disposed of by motion include a fully developed record of discovery, most of these terminations occur during the pleadings on grounds unrelated to discovery or its control. See appendix G for an analysis of discovery by types of disposition.

138. The t-values of 12.09 for settled cases and 7.08 for tried cases were both significant at the .001 level.

In the most-controlling courts, the average settled case was terminated 310 days earlier, and the average tried case, almost two years earlier than in the least-controlling courts.[139]

The combined effects of judge and court controls are shown in table 33. As expected, these data are consistent with the combined effects of controls on discovery time, shown in table 22 in the preceding chapter. Judges who use strong discovery controls will both settle and try cases faster than judges who use limited or no controls, independent of the control environment of the court. The court's control environment, however, has a marked effect.[140] Both judge-control groups realize shorter disposition times in courts with stronger control environments. The most dramatic evidence is the difference of two years (1,197 versus 440 days) between the average time for disposition of tried cases in the least-controlling courts before judges who use limited or no controls, and the average time in the most-controlling courts before judges who use strong controls.

TABLE 33

TOTAL DISPOSITION TIME BY EXTENT OF
COURT CONTROL AND JUDGE CONTROL, AND DISPOSITION TYPE
(Average Days)

| Disposition Type | Extent of Judge Control | Most-Controlling Courts | Moderate-Controlling Courts | Least-Controlling Courts |
|---|---|---|---|---|
| Settled | Strong | 312 | 389 | 489 |
|  | Limited or no | 564 | 597 | 768 |
| Tried | Strong | 440 | 552 | 756 |
|  | Limited or no | 751 | 720 | 1,197 |

Although tables 31 through 33 show a strong relationship between discovery time control and elapsed time for total case disposition, one cannot infer that the differences are caused by discovery controls alone. The differences in total case disposition time are much greater than the differences shown in chapter five for total discovery time. In chapter five, for example, the difference in total discovery time between judges using strong controls and those using limited or no controls was 158 days. For the same groups, the difference in total disposition time was 316 days for settled cases, and 473 days for tried cases. Differences between the

139. One-way analyses of variance yielded F-values of 50.6 and 42.7, respectively, for settled and tried cases. Both were significant at the .001 level.

140. Separate two-way analyses of variance for the settled- and tried-case populations yielded main effects for both court control and judge control, which were significant at the .001 level. Interaction effects were not significant.

effects of varying degrees of court control were similar. Thus, it is clear that the extent of control over discovery also affects the elapsed time for other stages of a case (non-discovery time).

### Contributions of Non-Discovery Time to Shortened Disposition Time

Observations of the courts during the data-collection period made it clear that discovery time controls are only part of a set of controls over all stages of a case. A sense of timely completion of discovery, where that sense exists, seems to pervade every stage of a case. Judges appear to be internally consistent; that is, they do not apply controls to isolated stages of a case. Instead, they establish a similar degree of judicial control over every stage of a case in preparation for trial. The relative degrees of control applied to discovery are also applied to the pleadings and pretrial stages.

Tables 34 and 35 show the results of these comprehensive controls. Table 34 contains aggregate information that shows, for all cases, the average number of days for non-discovery time (i.e., total disposition time minus total discovery time), related to the degree of judge and court control.[141] These data are broken into stage-by-stage time periods in table 35,[142] which permits comparisons of elapsed times for each of the first three stages in a case as these times relate to the degree of discovery control exerted by judges and the amount of discovery control in the court environment. The data confirm the comprehensive nature of judicial controls by showing quite clearly that other stages of a case are substantially affected by these controls.

TABLE 34

NON-DISCOVERY TIME BY JUDGE- AND COURT-CONTROL GROUPS
(Average Days)

| Judges Using Strong Controls | | Judges Using Limited or No Controls |
|---|---|---|
| 194 | | 382 |
| Most-Controlling Courts | Moderate-Controlling Courts | Least-Controlling Courts |
| 204 | 283 | 393 |

---

141. The t-value of 11.45, measuring the effect of judge control, is significant at the .001 level. The one-way analysis of variance measuring the effect of court control yielded an F-value of 46.5, which is significant at the .001 level.

142. The sum of these three stages will not add up to total disposition time: pleadings and discovery frequently overlap, and the elapsed time for the trial and posttrial stages are not included.

TABLE 35

DURATIONS OF STAGES OF LITIGATION
BY JUDGE- AND COURT-CONTROL GROUPS
(Average Days)

| Categories of Control | Pleadings | Discovery | Pretrial |
|---|---|---|---|
| Judges Using | | | |
| Strong controls | 116 | 176 | 126 |
| Limited or no controls | 180 | 334 | 296 |
| | | | |
| Court | | | |
| Most controlling | 122 | 185 | 140 |
| Moderate controlling | 166 | 249 | 178 |
| Least controlling | 163 | 347 | 315 |

Trial time data permit us to determine whether differences in that stage contributed to the shortening of total disposition time. In addition, those data permit us to ask one more question about the effects of control on discovery. We have seen that the number of discovery requests was unaffected by timing controls. We do not know whether the quality or quantity of exchanged information was affected. If there was an effect on information exchanged, one could expect some discernible difference in trial time, though the direction of the difference is not clear. More information might have increased trial time to allow introduction of more evidence. Conversely, more information might have eliminated issues at the pretrial stage, thereby shortening trial time. Both effects could operate simultaneously, cancelling observable differences, but that possibility is unlikely.

Data in table 36[143] show that trial time is unaffected by the degree of control over timing of discovery.[144] In all but one of the control categories, trial time averaged just over three days. Ideally, discovery control expedites discovery without affecting other aspects of the discovery process; these data on trial time suggest that the exchange of information remains unaffected.

## Pleadings and Discovery

We recognized the possibility that there might be an overlap between the pleadings stage and the discovery stage. Definitions of stages prevent overlaps between any other areas. Examination of data revealed that there

---

143. The total elapsed time for trials was not used because trials can span weekends, and continuances of trials might have distorted the results.

144. Analysis of variance disclosed no main effects and no interaction effects. There is still the possibility that contributions to the shortening of disposition time were made by reductions in the time during which bench trials are taken under advisement and in elapsed times for posttrial motions.

TABLE 36

TRIAL DURATIONS BY JUDGE- AND COURT-CONTROL GROUPS
(Average Days)

| | Most-Controlling Courts | Moderate-Controlling Courts | Least-Controlling Courts | All Courts |
|---|---|---|---|---|
| Cases before judges using strong controls | 3.3 | 3.2 | 3.2 | 3.3 |
| Cases before judges using limited or no controls | 2.4 | 3.3 | 3.3 | 3.2 |

are only minor overlaps between pleadings and discovery. Data obtained in
the study showed that filing of answers to original complaints and to subsequent claims is critical to the initiation of discovery. Attorneys in
cases subject to strong controls exhibited a slightly stronger tendency to
file discovery requests before all answers were filed, but responses were
rarely filed before the last answer. No significant differences on this
point were observed in cases subject to varying degrees of control. Accordingly, we conclude that discovery timing controls should be connected
to joinder of issue. This means, in turn, that the net benefit of shortened discovery time resulting from controls will depend on adherence to
rules governing time for answers to complaints, counterclaims, cross
claims, and third-party claims.

### Discovery and Pretrial

A judge cannot move a case into the pretrial stage unless the parties
have completed discovery.[145] Sometimes, the parties will need more time to
file discovery than the judge anticipated in setting the original cutoff
date. If so, the judge should allow additional time for this unanticipated
discovery.[146] But as is indicated below, that decision should be made on a
case-by-case basis, since automatic postponement extends discovery time
unnecessarily and may lead to delays in rescheduling subsequent events.

#### Postponement of the Discovery Cutoff Date

Imposing initial cutoff dates on a case-by-case basis will reduce the

---

145. A scarcity of judicial resources can affect the duration of the pretrial by decreasing the likelihood of trial. See, e.g., Aldisert, A Metropolitan Court Conquers Its Backlog, Part II: From Pure Pre-trial to Compulsory Settlement Conferences in Judicial Administration 217 (R. Wheeler &
H. Whitcomb eds. 1977). At the time of this study, only the judges in
Massachusetts indicated that lack of judge time was a problem. Consequently, in the following analysis, pretrial data for Massachusetts were not
studied.

146. See Freehill v. Lewis, 355 F.2d 46, 48 (4th Cir. 1966).

frequency of unanticipated discovery needs that require enlargement of the discovery period. The net result will be an overall reduction in total discovery time.

The best evidence for this proposition is found by comparing the data from the two most-controlling courts, Southern Florida and Central California. Florida judges set discovery cutoff dates on a case-by-case basis after appraising the likely discovery activity in each case. Postponement of the cutoff dates was granted only upon a showing of diligent effort and specific need before the cutoff date. In California, a local court rule establishes sixty days for completion of discovery in all cases. Postponements were much more common in California than in Florida; at least one was regularly granted, and frequently several were allowed. Perhaps because judges realized that the sixty-day cutoff is often unrealistic, attorneys usually were not required to show a need for more time.[147]

Our data show that, in Florida, 48 percent of cases with cutoff dates received one postponement, and 14 percent received multiple postponements. In Central California, these percentages were 85 and 60 percent, respectively. The higher percentage of single postponements in Central California was expected as a result of the uniform cutoff dates. The higher percentage of additional postponements, however, appears to be the result of the California enlargement policy, which does not require demonstration of need as a prerequisite for enlargement of the discovery control period.

Total discovery times in the two courts also exhibit substantial differences,[148] as shown in table 37.

TABLE 37

TOTAL DISCOVERY TIME BY DISCOVERY
VOLUME FOR SELECTED COURTS
(Average Days)

|  | Low Volume | Moderate Volume | High Volume | All Cases |
|---|---|---|---|---|
| S.Fla. | 53 | 126 | 395 | 150 |
| C.Cal. | 80 | 271 | 526 | 236 |

Discovery in Central California required about two months more than in Southern Florida. Of course, there are differences in the two courts beyond the discovery management practices noted here. Of the six courts

---

147. Some Central California judges delegated postponement authority, within certain guidelines, to deputy clerks. This policy appeared to have further reduced the necessity to make a showing of need for additional time.

148. Analysis of variance disclosed that main effects for both court control and volume were significant at the .001 level. The interaction effect was also significant at the .05 level.

studied, however, these two take the most similar general approach to controlling discovery time. We conclude, therefore, that much of the difference disclosed in table 37 should be attributed to their practices in setting dates and in granting enlargements of the discovery period.

## Scheduling the Final Pretrial Conference

Discovery timing control may affect the manner in which the final pretrial conference is scheduled, with a resulting impact on the length of the pretrial stage. In some courts, such as Southern Florida and Central California, the final pretrial conference was scheduled to be held about a week after the completion of discovery. Both the cutoff date for discovery and the final pretrial conference were scheduled in the same judicial order.

In Eastern Pennsylvania, the completion of discovery and the final pretrial conference were treated as separate events and were usually scheduled on an ad hoc basis. Since there was generally no control over discovery, the parties discovered at their own pace, and the judges depended on the attorneys to inform them about the completion of discovery. Often, however, completion of discovery was not announced until the judges scheduled semiannual or annual status conferences. If discovery was not completed, these status conferences did not advance the completion of discovery, since a simple assertion by attorneys that discovery was not complete usually turned the case back to them for further discovery. When the completion of discovery was ascertained, a final pretrial conference might not have been scheduled immediately because of the unavailability of judge time.

The effects of these different scheduling policies are shown by the data in table 38, which reports pretrial time for Southern Florida and Eastern Pennsylvania.

TABLE 38

DURATIONS OF DISCOVERY AND PRETRIAL STAGES
IN COMPLETED CASES FOR SELECTED COURTS
(Average Days)

| Stage | S.Fla. | E.Pa. |
|-----------|--------|-------|
| Discovery | 236 | 597 |
| Pretrial | 95 | 205 |

Although the use of settlement conferences by Eastern Pennsylvania judges surely had the effect of somewhat prolonging the pretrial stage, the four-month difference is more likely to result from failure of the parties to inform the judge of the status of the case.[149] Without cutoff dates, the judge cannot be aware of the completion of discovery until the next status conference. Unless status conferences are frequent, much time can pass before the judge learns of completion and sets a final pretrial conference. The Southern Florida judges, on the other hand, take the initiative in setting the cutoff and pretrial conference as soon as the pleadings close, thereby placing the burden on the parties to show the need for rescheduling these dates. This prevents the development of time gaps between the completion of discovery and the final pretrial conference.

## Limited Judicial Resources and the Use of Discovery Timing Controls

One final matter remains to be considered. Some judges have expressed concern about the advisability of holding lawyers to ambitious discovery schedules when the judges cannot find the time to try civil cases. Even after a case is fully discovered and ready for trial, demands of the Speedy Trial Act of 1974[150] and other factors[151] may not permit judges to maintain a credible threat of imminent civil trial, and without such a threat, cases that would otherwise settle may languish in the civil backlog.[152] Given this problem, some judges question the need to push for completion of discovery when there is no realistic prospect of trial. We believe that, notwithstanding the unavailability of trial time, the judge should still require completion of discovery as early as possible.

Discovery timing controls may not yield the shorter case disposition times shown in tables 31, 32, and 33, unless the judge can set a quick and realistic trial date. But if the speedy resolution of civil cases is a valued societal interest, providing sufficient judicial resources to dispose of civil cases is a matter that only Congress can resolve. Recent legislation may help some districts. Certainly, the omnibus judgeship legislation[153] will help return the civil trial calendars in some districts to current status. Also, United States magistrates can now be designated by

---

149. For the discovery stage, t-tests yielded a t-value of 4.75, which was significant at the .001 level. For the pretrial stage, the t-value of 3.05 was significant at the .01 level.

150. 18 U.S.C. §§ 3161 to 3174 (Supp. 1978).

151. E.g., an unusually heavy workload, long trials, illness, unfilled judgeships, etc.

152. The relationship between the threat of imminent trial and settlements has been identified by many judges as a crucial factor in settling cases. See, e.g., Aldisert, supra note 145.

153. H.R. 7843, 95th Cong., 2d Sess., 124 Cong. Rec. S1335, H717 (daily ed. Feb. 7, 1978).

judges to try certain civil cases, if the parties consent.[154] Any sudden availability of judge time, however, might be wasted if a new judge or a visiting judge had to first prepare an old case for trial by scheduling the completion of discovery.

Even if adequate resources cannot be provided to try civil cases promptly, a better factual presentation can be made when the case is finally tried if discovery activity is completed as soon as possible. Over time, witnesses' recollections fade, and vital documents can be lost. An important policy behind the statute of limitations is to ensure that evidence is captured by discovery before it deteriorates.[155] To be consistent with that policy, discovery activity ought not to be permitted to linger simply because of dim prospects for an early trial. Moreover, to the extent that full information promotes settlement, early completion of discovery may accelerate cases that will terminate without trial. Thus, we conclude that, independent of the valid concerns over availability of trial days, there are sufficiently good reasons to control the timing of discovery.

---

154. 28 U.S.C. § 636 (Supp. 1977).

155. Order of R.R. Telegraphers v. Railway Express Agency, Inc., 321 U.S. 342, 348-49 (1944):

> Statutes of limitation, . . . in their conclusive effects are designed to promote justice by preventing surprises through the revival of claims that have been allowed to slumber until evidence has been lost, memories have faded, and witnesses have disappeared.

CHAPTER VII

## MODEL FOR EFFECTIVE DISCOVERY CONTROL

Effective control over the pace of discovery depends upon judicial management exercised primarily under provisions of rule 83 of the Federal Rules of Civil Procedure. Judicial controls should not be rigid or mechanistic; they should have a relationship to the discovery requirements of each case.

Discovery is, of course, only one aspect of litigation. The benefits that can flow from judicial control of discovery time can be fully realized only through a comprehensive case management system governing every stage of the litigation process. Recommended methods of effective case management have been taught in Federal Judicial Center seminars for newly appointed district judges since the creation of the Center in 1967, and before that at seminars started in 1961 under the leadership of Judge Alfred P. Murrah, director of the Center from May, 1970, through October, 1974. These procedures and control systems are described in Federal Judicial Center seminar proceedings. [156]

The recommended model described herein bears strong similarities to those systems. However, the recommendations in this report are different in two ways. First, they are derived from the research data collected in this study. Second, since the data analysis in this report is limited primarily to the discovery process, the recommendations are also limited primarily to the discovery stage of civil cases.

### Element 1: Selecting Control Tracks
The judge should place civil cases on either a motion control or a discovery control track.

The first management decision is selecting the appropriate control track. The choice between a discovery control track and a motion control track can be informed by reference to the subject matter of the case, revealed in the pleadings.

Prisoner cases, administrative appeals cases, and seizure cases are prime candidates for the motion track. These areas of litigation rarely generate issues of fact and are usually terminated by motion. Such cases

---

156. See note 56 supra.

do not benefit from discovery controls; motion controls should be invoked. Motion control requires establishing a schedule by which motions and answers to motions are due.[157] In the exceptional case, in which discovery is needed, a party could request that the case be taken off the motion track, and the judge could then consider whether to invoke discovery controls.[158]

For cases in other areas of litigation, we recommend placing the case on a discovery control track. It should be noted, however, that some extraordinary cases may best be handled through procedures suggested in the Manual for Complex Litigation.

### Element 2:  Setting Controls Over the Case

The judge should invoke judicial controls as soon as the issues are joined.

Most judges who use strong discovery timing controls invoke them either before or at joinder; a few judges choose to delay setting the discovery cutoff date until after discovery is under way.

Delaying imposition of timing controls would be necessary if discovery requirements were so erratic that reasonable estimates could not be made. In that circumstance, early imposition would result in a proliferation of enlargement motions that would waste both the judge's and the attorneys' time. In practice, however, the amount of discovery activity does not vary as much as is commonly believed, nor is the amount as large as is commonly believed. At joinder of issue, controls can be invoked with sufficient accuracy to avoid frequent need for enlargement of the allotted time period. Characteristics of the pleadings provide important aids in accurately estimating discovery activity.

Setting controls before joinder risks wasting time[159] and does not

---

157. Prisoner cases filed under 42 U.S.C. § 1983 (1970), particularly because of the high incidence of pro se representation, present distinctive management problems requiring special responses. See Federal Judicial Center, Recommended Procedures for Handling Prisoner Civil Rights Cases in The Federal Courts (Tentative Report No. 2) (1977).

158. The order scheduling motion activity could announce the party's right to request this switch, and it could even set a cutoff date for such a request.

159. Time can be wasted in two ways. First, the pleadings can be unpredictable; the joinder of issue can be delayed by difficulty in effecting service of process, rulings on motions, amendments to the pleadings, and the addition of other claims. If joinder were delayed, the cutoff date would require postponement, using up the judge's and attorneys' time. Second, substantial numbers of cases are settled, voluntarily dismissed, or terminated by motion before the joinder of issue. For these cases, the imposition of controls would be a waste of judges' time.

provide a good vantage point for considering the predictors of discovery use.[160]  Setting controls at joinder of issue eliminates these problems, giving the judge a chance to use all the predictors in the pleadings, thereby decreasing the likelihood of enlargement requests.

Joinder of issue occurs at different times in different cases.  Most cases involve one plaintiff and one defendant, with one complaint and one answer.  For these cases, the issue is joined when the answer is filed, and discovery timing controls should be imposed shortly thereafter.  Cases with several defendants, but no pleadings other than their answers, are fully joined when the last answer is filed.  Cases involving several defendants, third-party defendants, or intervenors can develop complex pleadings by the filing of counterclaims, cross claims, and third-party claims.  The appropriate time to impose discovery timing controls will depend on the structure of the pleadings.  The objective is to invoke controls _after_ the pleadings have established the controversy.

Consider, for example, the filing of a counterclaim.  Rule 13 requires the defendant to file counterclaims with the answer; the judge will be aware of counterclaims when the original issues between the parties are joined.  This early notice permits postponing timing controls until the counterclaim is controverted without adversely affecting the overall control pattern.  Discovery controls are most effectively applied after that time because (1) parties do not usually begin discovery until after claims are controverted, (2) challenges to the sufficiency of a counterclaim may introduce unpredictable variables, and (3) a controverted counterclaim is a useful predictor of increased discovery activity.

Cross claims present similar considerations.  Joinder should not be deemed complete until answers to cross claims have been filed.

Third-party defendants or intervenors may or may not appear in a case, and they may appear at varying times.  Such uncertain events should not delay the imposition of discovery timing controls.  If additional parties or claims appear, previously imposed controls can be modified as soon as the claims have been controverted and probable discovery needs have been assessed.

No model can address every situation that may arise, and no amount of data will substitute for the judge's experience.  Basic principles, however, can guide case-by-case decisions even in the exceptional situation.  The basic principle of this element is that discovery timing controls should be applied to all claims as soon as they have been controverted.

---

160.  Counterclaims, cross claims, and parties added to the controversy by third-party complaints could not be considered for prediction purposes if controls were imposed early in the pleadings.

## Element 3:  Setting the Discovery Cutoff Date

Maximal use of allotted time and m i n i m a l
administrative costs are obtained by predicting the duration according to the
pleadings characteristics of each case.


The central element of effective discovery control is setting appropriate durations for discovery.  Two competing interests must be weighed
in this process.  Too much time removes the incentive for prompt initiation
of discovery.  Too little time increases the burden of motions to enlarge
the control period.  The ideal setting should strike a balance between
these competing interests.

Two different approaches to setting cutoff dates were considered:
standard and case-by-case settings.  Although standard periods are easily
fixed in the initial stage of discovery, a standard time that meets all
needs appears elusive.  Establishing cutoff dates on a case-by-case basis,
according to the nature of the pleadings, may require some early administrative effort, but it appears to strike the critical balance better than
any other observed system.  We therefore recommend that upon joinder of issue, the judge set cutoff dates according to the needs of each individual
case.

How much discovery time should the parties be allotted?  The experience of the judge is the prime asset in this process.  Certain case characteristics may suggest the probability that few requests will be filed and
the parties will need only a short time to complete discovery; other case
characteristics may indicate the likelihood of more requests and the need
for substantial discovery time.

The judge can be aided in this task by the findings in this report.
Certain characteristics of the pleadings were found to be reliable predictors of discovery activity.  These are the subject matter of the controversy, the number of parties, and the presence of controverted counterclaims
or controverted cross claims.  We recommend that the judge consider these
characteristics in predicting the number of requests in cases.  The following formula reports the number of requests for the paradigm case[161] and the
increase in requests that can be expected by the presence of each case
characteristic.[162]

---

161.  The paradigm case had two parties and no pleadings other than a
complaint and an answer, and was of a type not listed in note 164 infra.

162.  The "amount in controversy" characteristic was not included in the
multiple regression used to calculate the increases reported in this
chapter, but it was included in the calculations reported in chapter four.
As a consequence, the values reported here differ slightly from those
reported in the earlier chapter.  See note 96 supra.

Predicted requests[163] = A + B + C + D + E, where:

A = 3.6 requests as a base (the paradigm case);

B = 1.1 requests times the number of parties over two (otherwise 0);

C = 2.3 requests if the case is in a "high volume" case-type category (otherwise 0);[164]

D = 2.1 requests if the case has a controverted counterclaim (otherwise 0); and

E = 2.7 requests if the case has a controverted cross claim (otherwise 0).

Two examples will illustrate the use of this formula. First, assume the pleadings show two parties, a controversy arising from an auto accident, and no controverted counterclaim by the defendant. In that case, the estimate would be 3.6 requests: 3.6 as a base, 0 for the parties, 0 for the case type, 0 for counterclaims, and 0 for cross claims.

Second, assume the pleadings reveal that a case has four parties, the subject of the controversy is alleged medical malpractice, and no controverted counterclaims or cross claims have been filed. The estimate for the case would be 8.1 discovery requests: 3.6 as a base, 2.2 for the two parties over the minimum of two, and 2.3 for the "high volume" case type.

Once requests are predicted, the judge must allot sufficient time to complete discovery. This task may be aided by reference to time used by attorneys to discover in the most-controlling court. The actual time needed to discover in that environment may be a useful benchmark in setting realistic cutoff dates.

Table 39 displays the average discovery times for varying numbers of requests, rounded to the nearest 30-day interval. For the two cases illustrating the use of the formula, the allotment would be 120 days for the first case with its 3.6 requests, and 150 days for the second, with 8.1 requests.[165]

---

163. The F-values associated with the beta coefficient were significant at the .001 level. All predictors combined accounted for 16% of the variance.

164. The "high volume" case types are: tort--product liability; patent; contract--franchise; contract--warranty; tort--malpractice (legal/medical); Jones Act and seaman's injury; tort--airline; trade regulation; securities; tort--slip and fall; contract--realty; tort--miscellaneous (for a definition of this case type, see note 103 supra).

165. The accuracy of the estimating process was tested by comparing estimates of time based on the characteristics of the most-controlling court's cases and the actual discovery times for the same cases. The results showed that the system underestimated time in 27% of the settings, meaning that initial enlargement would be needed in about one out of four settings. This would be a 21% improvement over the 48% of initial enlargements in that court for the sampled cases. As shown by the figures below, employing

TABLE 39

AVERAGE DISCOVERY TIMES BY NUMBER OF REQUESTS
IN THE MOST-CONTROLLING COURT

| Requests | Discovery Times[a] |
|----------|-------------------|
| 4,5 | 120 days |
| 6,7,8 | 150 days |
| 9 and over | 180 days |

[a]Rounded to the nearest 30-day interval.

We recommend that a minimum of 120 days and a maximum of 180 days be allotted for discovery. The judge might consider allotting less than 120 days if the controversy will clearly not generate four requests. More than 180 days, however, should not be provided at the initial setting even if there are indications that the case will have more than nine requests. Should discovery activity actually require more than six months, the parties will surely seek an enlargement, and this will give the judge a chance to set a new date based on the progress made during the previous six months and assess the remaining needs. Otherwise, if the time provided is longer than needed, and there is not a six-month limit, case disposition may be needlessly delayed.[166]

> Element 4: Enlarging the Control Period
> Postponements of the cutoff date should be granted only if the moving party shows both active discovery during the initial control period and a specific need for further discovery.

The integrity of the discovery control system is dependent in large part on the policy of the judge towards enlargements. If the parties anticipate routine postponements of the original cutoff date, its effectiveness in advancing the completion of discovery will be seriously undermined. On the other hand, overly rigid enforcement may impair the right to

---

the same test for cases in the other courts, 48% of the cases overall would have required initial enlargements, meaning that in 52% of these cases, use of this estimating process would not have required the parties to discover at a faster pace than they already did, frequently without any discovery controls.

| S.Fla. | C.Cal. | Md. | E.La. | E.Pa. | Mass. | All Courts |
|--------|--------|-----|-------|-------|-------|------------|
| 27% | 47% | 50% | 49% | 55% | 65% | 48% |

166. As noted in the discussion under Element 1, the controls suggested in the Manual for Complex Litigation would be appropriate for multidistrict or unusually complex cases.

use discovery devices provided by rule 26(b). The optimum enlargement system, therefore, must strike a balance between these competing interests.

Differing enlargement policies affect the effectiveness of discovery timing controls. Routine postponements of the cutoff date provide the parties with sufficient time to discover, but work against the other important interest of control--getting the parties to use efficiently the time allotted for discovery. The result is delay in completing discovery and slippage in the holding of the final pretrial conference.

The better policy requires the attorneys to persuade the court that they have actively undertaken discovery during the original control period or that there is good cause for inactivity. The moving party must also show with some specificity that more discovery time is needed. This policy promotes the efficient use of the initial control period, reduces the number of enlargement motions, and provides sufficient time to complete discovery.

If a court decides to permit an enlargement of the control period, a decision about the appropriate duration must then be made. The judge should be aided in that decision by the parties' statements of their specific discovery needs. If the parties need only a few additional discovery exchanges, a new cutoff date and a commensurate date for the final pretrial conference should be set. If the issues are so complex that further discovery needs cannot be estimated, enlargements by sixty-day increments would ensure continued active discovery.

One final point about enlargements should be made. A hearing on these motions ordinarily need not be held. Virtually all such motions can be handled "on the papers." A ruling can usually be made by a quick review of the docket sheet and the grounds for additional discovery time set forth in the motion.

### Element 5: Terminating the Discovery Period

The termination of the discovery period should be shortly before the final pretrial conference. Both dates should be set in a single order to put the attorneys on notice that the court intends to enforce the discovery cutoff date.

Once the cutoff date has been reached, it is important that the court maintain control of the case.[167] Simultaneous scheduling of the next event--the final pretrial conference--provides a built-in termination of the discovery period.

---

167. See generally M. Solomon, Case Flow Management in the Trial Court, 2 ABA Commission on Standards of Judicial Administration (1973).

Courts using the strongest controls schedule the holding of the final pretrial conference for shortly after the cutoff date and announce both dates in the same scheduling order. Scheduling the final pretrial conference in the same order as the invocation of the discovery cutoff date provides an automatic transition from discovery to the pretrial stage of the case. Gaps of inactivity between the two stages are thereby minimized, and the court can promptly set the case for trial.[168]

### Element 6: Implementing the Discovery Control System
The discovery timing control system is best embodied in a local rule.

Under rule 83, controls may be promulgated either by local rule applicable to the whole court or by standing order applicable to a single judge or a group of judges. Although the rule provides no guidance on the relative merits of local rules and standing orders, from a case management standpoint, establishment of the discovery timing control system by local rule has distinct advantages over establishment through standing orders.

The adoption of a local rule is an announcement to the bar that the court has made a significant policy decision and that uniform compliance is expected.[169] The use of a local rule will also increase the efficiency of the system itself. By codifying the procedure in a form accessible to all federal practitioners, judges will spend less time teaching lawyers their individual control policies. Attorneys who generally practice in the state courts or in another jurisdiction may be unaware of standing orders. A local rule, however, gives lawyers notice of the court's use of discovery controls long before a case is filed. Earlier notice may eliminate the need for attorneys to accelerate discovery in reaction to a standing order, by allowing them to plan discovery from the very outset of the controversy.

It must be noted, however, that the court with the most effective system of discovery controls operates with standing orders. Even so, if the court is perceived to have a uniform control policy, enforcement problems will be minimized. Therefore, in the absence of significant policy differences among the judges, even a highly effective court is likely to benefit from promulgating a local rule to embody its discovery control system.

---

168. It may also be advisable for the court to require the attorneys to file motions to postpone the cutoff date or the final pretrial conference, sufficiently in advance to allow processing of such motions without upsetting the court's calendar.

169. This is not to suggest an excessively detailed rule (see, e.g., McCargo v. Hedrick, 545 F.2d 393 (4th Cir. 1976)) but rather, a more general rule that includes the other five elements recommended in this chapter.

# APPENDIX A

## SAMPLING METHODOLOGY

The District Court Studies Project examined six metropolitan courts[170] with sharply contrasting numbers of terminations per judgeship and times for case dispositions to ascertain whether the procedures used in those courts accounted for the statistical differences. With one exception, all six courts were selected on the basis of their fiscal 1973 performance; Massachusetts was selected based on its fiscal 1974-75 statistics. Table 40 shows the statistical ranking of the six courts among the twenty-four metropolitan courts; figure 7 shows the standing of these six courts regarding time and number of case dispositions. The data used in this report were collected in each of the six courts; they pertain to approximately 500 randomly selected civil cases, each terminated in fiscal 1975.[171] (Additional information on these courts is provided in tables 41 and 42, which contain statistical portraits of various performance measures.)

The information collected for each case included the dates of all recorded actions taken by counsel or the court.[172] First the case file was examined, then the docket sheet was reviewed to validate the dates recorded and ensure the completeness of the file.[173]

---

170. A metropolitan court is roughly defined as one with six or more judgeships. Metropolitan courts, as opposed to smaller ones, were studied because: they are large enough to soften the impact of any individual judge; their case loads tend to be diverse, assuring that a broad cross section of federal litigation is represented in the sample; and their number is likely to increase in the future, as the federal court system grows.

171. Certain types of cases were systematically excluded. Mutidistrict litigation cases, uncontested Federal Home Loan Act and Veterans Home Loan Act collection cases, and cases enforcing foreign subpoenas were excluded from the sample. Multidistrict cases frequently did not have a full set of case filings; the other two types of cases usually had no filings or docket sheet entries. In addition, cases on appeal and certain other cases were excluded if the files were unavailable. If a randomly selected case was excluded, the immediately preceding case on the termination list was substituted. Interstate Commerce Commission (ICC) cases in Massachusetts were excluded because of their singularly high rate of filing in that court. ICC cases do not tap judicial resources in a proportionate way in that district, since practically all such cases are handled by one deputy clerk.

172. The data collection instrument is in appendix B.

173. The filing date recorded by the clerk's office was used unless there was a discrepancy of more than three days between the filing date and counsel's mailing date. In such cases, the mailing date was used to obtain a more accurate record of the time in which counsel had acted. If filings appeared to be missing, correspondence between counsel and the court was examined to determine if any reference to the missing filing was made.

## TABLE 40

## TIME AND NUMBER OF DISPOSITIONS PER JUDGESHIP OF METROPOLITAN DISTRICT COURTS

| Civil Median Time (months) | | | | Dispositions per Judgeship | | | | Criminal Median Time (months) | | | |
|---|---|---|---|---|---|---|---|---|---|---|---|
| Courts | '73 | '74 | '75 | Courts | '73 | '74 | '75 | Courts | '73 | '74 | '75 |
| S.Fla.* | 4 | 4 | 4 | E.La.* | 535 | 465 | 453 | S.C. | 2.5 | 2.3 | 3.0 |
| W.Tex. | 5 | 7 | 10 | E.Va. | 516 | 463 | 527 | W.Tex. | 2.5 | 3.0 | 2.8 |
| M.Fla. | 6 | 8 | 7 | N.Tex. | 487 | 471 | 434 | S.Cal. | 2.6 | 2.8 | 2.9 |
| N.Ill. | 6 | 6 | 6 | Ariz. | 487 | 444 | 458 | E.Va. | 2.8 | 2.4 | 2.4 |
| Ariz. | 7 | 7 | 8 | S.Cal. | 478 | 539 | 607 | E.La.* | 2.9 | 2.7 | 2.4 |
| C.Cal.* | 7 | 7 | 7 | S.Tex. | 453 | 455 | 415 | N.Tex. | 2.9 | 3.0 | 2.8 |
| E.Va. | 7 | 7 | 7 | M.Fla. | 448 | 398 | 416 | S.Tex. | 2.9 | 3.4 | 5.6 |
| N.Tex. | 7 | 9 | 10 | N.Ga. | 441 | 467 | 536 | S.Fla.* | 3.0 | 3.2 | 3.1 |
| S.Cal. | 8 | 7 | 10 | N.Tex. | 439 | 435 | 450 | C.Cal.* | 3.3 | 3.5 | 3.3 |
| N.Ga. | 8 | 6 | 7 | S.Fla.* | 435 | 402 | 447 | Ariz. | 3.4 | 3.2 | 3.0 |
| S.C. | 8 | 6 | 6 | S.C. | 430 | 422 | 547 | N.Ga. | 4.0 | 4.1 | 4.5 |
| E.N.Y. | 9 | 10 | 11 | D.C. | 407 | 263 | 193 | N.Ohio | 4.6 | 3.4 | 3.4 |
| D.C. | 10 | 8 | 7 | N.Ohio | 369 | 343 | 370 | N.Cal. | 4.9 | 4.4 | 4.0 |
| N.Ohio | 10 | 10 | 8 | Mass.* | 368 | 540 | 667 | N.Ill. | 5.5 | 5.2 | 5.1 |
| E.Mich. | 10 | 9 | 9 | S.N.Y. | 365 | 325 | 294 | Md.* | 5.7 | 5.6 | 4.5 |
| W.Pa. | 10 | 9 | 8 | E.Mich. | 357 | 339 | 393 | M.Fla. | 5.8 | 4.5 | 4.6 |
| S.Tex. | 10 | 12 | 11 | Md.* | 325 | 292 | 332 | E.Mich. | 5.8 | 6.3 | 6.8 |
| E.La.* | 11 | 11 | 10 | N.Ill. | 325 | 315 | 337 | E.N.Y. | 6.8 | 6.4 | 6.2 |
| Md.* | 11 | 10 | 9 | N.Cal. | 319 | 320 | 334 | S.N.Y. | 6.8 | 5.7 | 5.8 |
| N.Cal. | 12 | 12 | 11 | E.N.Y. | 308 | 321 | 300 | E.Pa.* | 7.0 | 4.3 | 4.2 |
| Mass.* | 12 | 18 | 19 | C.Cal.* | 307 | 304 | 563 | W.Pa. | 7.0 | 5.8 | 6.0 |
| E.Pa.* | 17 | 16 | 12 | N.J. | 260 | 276 | 323 | Mass.* | 7.6 | 8.4 | 7.6 |
| N.J. | 10 | 12 | 13 | E.Pa.* | 237 | 234 | 250 | D.C. | 7.7 | 5.7 | 3.7 |
| S.N.Y. | 25 | 18 | 15 | W.Pa. | 176 | 167 | 172 | N.J. | 11.7 | 12.7 | 12.2 |

Note: The courts are ranked by their performance in fiscal 1973. The six courts selected for study are identified by asterisks.

FIGURE 7

RELATIVE STANDING OF SIX METROPOLITAN
DISTRICT COURTS

| | "Speed" | |
| | Fast — Slow | |
|---|---|---|
| "Productivity" High | Southern District of Florida (S.Fla.) | Eastern District of Louisiana (E.La.)a Massachusetts (Mass.)b |
| Low | Central District of California (C.Cal.) | Eastern District of Pennsylvania (E.Pa.) Maryland (Md.) |

Source:  Case Management report, supra note 7, figure 1 at 3.

aCivil cases only; disposition of criminal cases is faster than most.

bIncludes ICC cases that require negligible judge attention.  Exclusive of those cases, Massachusetts productivity figures have been near the national average.

## TABLE 41

### FISCAL 1973 STATISTICAL PORTRAIT OF SIX METROPOLITAN COURTS SELECTED FOR STUDY

| | S.Fla.[b] No. / Rank | | C.Cal.[b] No. / Rank | | Md.[b] No. / Rank | | E.La.[b] No. / Rank | | E.Pa.[b] No. / Rank | | Mass.[a] No. / Rank[b] | |
|---|---|---|---|---|---|---|---|---|---|---|---|---|
| Number of judgeships | 7 | | 16 | | 7 | | 9 | | 19 | | 6 | |
| Total filings in fiscal 1973 | 3,081 | | 5,301 | | 2,008 | | 4,142 | | 3,582 | | 1,940 | |
| **Statistics per judgeship** | | | | | | | | | | | | |
| Filings (civil) | 310 | (8) | 195 | (20) | 196 | (19) | 391 | (1) | 152 | (22) | 261 | (9) |
| Pending cases | 135 | (22) | 170 | (20) | 192 | (16) | 398 | (2) | 226 | (11) | 488 | (1) |
| Terminations | 306 | (8) | 178 | (21) | 233 | (12) | 463 | (1) | 188 | (19) | 148 | (22) |
| Trials completed (civil and criminal) | 73 | (3) | 49 | (12) | 46 | (14) | 62 | (7) | 33 | (20) | 24 | (24) |
| Median time from filing to disposition (civil) | 4 mos. | (1) | 7 mos. | (5) | 11 mos. | (20) | 11 mos. | (19) | 17 mos. | (23) | 12 mos. | (21)[c] |
| Median time from issue to trial (civil) | 5 mos. | (2) | 10 mos. | (6) | 11 mos. | (7) | 17 mos. | (17) | 29 mos. | (24) | 17 mos. | (17)[c] |
| Number and percentage of civil cases over 3 years old | 26 2.8% | (4) | 175 6.5% | (13) | 120 9% | (20) | 182 5.1% | (9) | 532 12.4% | (22) | 226 3.3% | (6) |

See p. 90 for notes to table.

TABLE 42

FISCAL 1975 STATISTICAL PORTRAIT OF SIX METROPOLITAN
COURTS SELECTED FOR STUDY

| | S.Fla. No. | Rank[b] | C.Cal. No. | Rank[b] | Md. No. | Rank[b] | E.La. No. | Rank[b] | E.Pa. No. | Rank[b] | Mass.[a] No. | Rank[b] |
|---|---|---|---|---|---|---|---|---|---|---|---|---|
| Number of judgeships | 7 | | 16 | | 7 | | 9 | | 19 | | 6 | |
| Total filings in fiscal 1973 | 3,694 | | 6,270 | | 2,529 | | 4,551 | | 4,319 | | 2,524 | |
| Statistics per judgeship | | | | | | | | | | | | |
| Filings (civil) | 408 | ( 4) | 268 | (11) | 237 | (16) | 423 | ( 3) | 186 | (21) | 321 | ( 9) |
| Pending cases | 206 | (20) | 231 | (15) | 207 | (19) | 442 | ( 2) | 195 | (21) | 624 | ( 1) |
| Terminations | 341 | ( 5) | 237 | (15) | 218 | (16) | 377 | ( 3) | 189 | (21) | 242 | (14) |
| Trials completed (civil and criminal) | 71 | ( 4) | 37 | (17) | 48 | (12) | 55 | (10) | 33 | (21) | 30 | (23) |
| Median time from filing to disposition (civil) | 4 mos. | ( 1) | 7 mos. | ( 4) | 9 mos. | (12) | 10 mos. | (14) | 12 mos. | (21) | 19 mos. | (24)[c] |
| Median time from issue to trial (civil) | 5 mos. | ( 1) | 12 mos. | (10) | 11 mos. | ( 9) | 13 mos. | (12) | 18 mos. | (20) | 26 mos. | (24)[c] |
| Number and percentage of civil cases over 3 years old | 15 1.2% | ( 1) | 256 7.0% | (17) | 84 5.9% | (13) | 115 2.9% | ( 3) | 178 4.8% | ( 9) | 931 9.0% | (20) |

See p. 90 for notes to table.

90

Notes to tables 41 and 42

Source:  Administrative Off. U.S. Courts, Management Statistics for United States Courts 1973 and 1975.

aFiles relating to ICC regulations have been eliminated from the sample.

bThe rankings are based on the position of each court among the 24 metropolitan trial courts.

cICC cases are included in these median figures.

FEDERAL JUDICIAL CENTER
CIVIL CASE CODING SHEET

Serial No.*(1)* _____
Type*(6)* HEAD Ref. No.*(10)* 01
Form*(12)*: _____ of*(13)* _____ forms

Disregard*(14)* [ ]

Collector's Initials _____
  (Code*(15)* ____ )

A. COURT/DIV.: _____ COURT CODE*(16)*: _____

B. DOCKET NO.*(20)*: _____ JUDGE: _____ JUDGE CODE*(26)*: _____

C. PLAINTIFFS: P1: _____ P. ATTY. CODE *(30)*: _____
              P2: _____ P. ATTY. CODE *(40)*: _____
              P3: _____ P. ATTY. CODE *(50)*: _____

D. DEFENDANTS: D1: _____ D. ATTY. CODE *(60)*: _____
              D2: _____ D. ATTY. CODE *(70)*: _____
              D3: _____ D. ATTY. CODE *(80)*: _____

E. THIRD PARTY
   DEFENDANTS: T1: _____ T. ATTY. CODE *(90)*: _____
              T2: _____ T. ATTY. CODE*(100)*: _____

F. INTERVENORS: I1: _____ I. ATTY. CODE*(110)*: _____
               I2: _____ I. ATTY. CODE*(120)*: _____

G. AMOUNT IN CONTROVERSY*(130)*: _____ H. CASE TYPE: _____ CODE*(137)*: ___

I. FACTS (ISSUES AND COMMENTS): _____

   _____

J. DATE CONTROVERSY AROSE*(140-145)*: _____

K. DATE SUBSTANTIAL COMPLETION OF DISCOVERY*(146-151)*: _____

II. PLEADINGS

TYPES: CCLM - Counter Claim
       COMP - Complaint
       CRCL - Cross Claim
       TPCP - Third Party Complaint

CODES: By: P1, P2, D1, D2, etc.
       Versus: P1, P2, D1, D2, etc.
       Compulsory: Y-Yes, N-No
       Informative: 1-10
       Germane: 1-10

Service by Marshal:  Y-Yes, N-No
Service Type: M-Mail, C-Constructive,
             P-Personal, N-Newspaper

| TYPE | REF. NO. | DATE | BY | VERSUS | COMPULSORY (CCLM only) | INFORMATIVE (COMP or TPCP) | SERVICE OF PROCESS | | | TYPE | ANSWER | |
|------|------|------|------|------|------|------|------|------|------|------|------|------|
| | | | | | | | FIRST ATTEMPT DATE | COMPLETED DATE | BY MARSHAL | | DATE | GERMANE (COMP, TPCP) |
| *6-9* | *10-11* | *12-17* | *18-19* | *20-21* | *22* | *23-24* | *25-30* | *31-36* | *37* | *38* | *39-44* | *45-46* |
| | | | | | | | | | | | | |
| | | | | | | | | | | | | |
| | | | | | | | | | | | | |
| | | | | | | | | | | | | |
| | | | | | | | | | | | | |

III. AMENDMENTS

CODES: By: P1, P2, D1, D2, etc.
       Versus: P1, P2, D1, D2, etc.
       Service Type: M-Mail, P-Personal, C-Constructive, N-Newspaper (publication)
       Answer Needed: Y-Yes, N-No
       Service by Marshal   Y-Yes, N-No

| TYPE | REF. NO. | CROSS REFERENCE | | DATE | BY | VERSUS | SERVICE OF PROCESS | | | TYPE | ANSWER NEEDED | ANSWER DATE |
|------|------|------|------|------|------|------|------|------|------|------|------|------|
| | | TYPE | REF.NO. | | | | FIRST ATTEMPT DATE | COMPLETED DATE | BY MARSHAL | | | |
| *6-9* | *10-11* | *12-15* | *14-17* | *18-23* | *24-25* | *26-27* | *28-33* | *34-39* | *40* | *41* | *42* | *43-46* |
| AMEN | | | | | | | | | | | | |
| AMEN | | | | | | | | | | | | |
| AMEN | | | | | | | | | | | | |
| AMEN | | | | | | | | | | | | |
| AMEN | | | | | | | | | | | | |

IV. DISCOVERY

TYPES:
DEPO - Depositions
INTR - Interrogatories
LTDP - Motion for Leave to Take Deposition of
       Person Departing District
ORED - Motion for Order Regarding Expenses of
       Deposition
PMEX - Motion for Physical or Mental Examination

MSDM - Miscellaneous Discovery Motions
PRIR - Motion for Protective Order
QUAS - Quash
RPDC - Request for Production of Documents
RQAD - Request for Admission
SPDT - Subpoena Duces Tecum
TLED - Motion to Terminate or Limit Examination
       on Deposition
WQST - Written Questions

CODES:
By: P1, D1, JD-Judge, MG-Magistrate
To: P1, D1, etc.
Of: U-Unknown, W-Witness, E-Expert Witness,
    C-Custodian of Records, P-Party, D-Doctor
Brief: No. of Briefs
Surname: Rating 1-10

## V. SUBSTANTIVE MOTIONS

TYPES:
- DEJD – Default Judgment
- DEJP – Dismiss for Failure to Join a Party
- DFSC – Dismiss for Failure to State Claim
- DIMV – Dismiss for Improper Venue
- DLPJ – Dismiss for Lack of Personal Jurisdiction
- DLSM – Dismiss for Lack of Subject Matter Jurisdiction
- DSPR – Dismiss for Insufficient Service of Process

- FPRO – Failure to Prosecute
- JDPL – Judgment on Pleadings
- MDST – More Definite Statement
- MSSM – Miscellaneous Substantive Motions
- PRMJ – Preliminary Injunction
- STRK – Strike
- SUJD – Summary Judgment
- TMRO – Temporary Restraining Order

CODES:
By: P1, P2, JD–Judge, MG–Magistrate
Versus: D1, D2, etc.
Brief (1–10)
What: C–Complaint, A–Answer, I–Answer to Interrogatory; V –Affidavits, O–Other

| TYPE | REF. NO. | MOTION | | | | | | | WHAT STRK only | MOTION TO DISSOLVE (TMRO and PRMJ only) | | | | | | DESCRIPTION MSSM only |
| | | DATE | BT | VERSUS | BRIEF Excluding STRK | ANSWER | | | | DATE | BY | VERSUS | BRIEF | ANSWER | | |
| | | | | | | DATE | BRIEF | | | | | | | DATE | BRIEF | |
| 6-9 | 10-11 | 13-17 | 18-19 | 20-21 | 22-23 | 24-28 | 30-31 | 32 | | 33-38 | 39-40 | 41-42 | 43-44 | 45-50 | 51-52 | |
| | | | | | | | | | | | | | | | | |
| | | | | | | | | | | | | | | | | |
| | | | | | | | | | | | | | | | | |
| | | | | | | | | | | | | | | | | |
| | | | | | | | | | | | | | | | | |
| | | | | | | | | | | | | | | | | |

## VI. JUDICIAL RESPONSES

CODES:
Action: G–Granted, D–Denied, P–Partial W–Withdrawn
Subtype: O–Original, C–Compel, S–Sanctions D–Dissolve,

| TYPE | REF. NO. | CROSS REFERENCE (Except CONT, ENLG, EXTN–see VIII) | | | NOTICE OF HEARING | | DATE HEARING HELD | RULING | | | NO. OF PAGES OF MEMO ORDER | DATE OF ORDER TO VACATE |
| | | TYPE | REF. NO. | SUBTYPE | DATE | DATE SET | | DATE | ACTION | DATE SET FOR ANSWER | | |
| 6-9 | 10-11 | 12-15 | 16-17 | 18 | 19-24 | 25-30 | 31-36 | 37-42 | 43 | 44-49 | 50-51 | 52-57 |
| JUDR | | | | | | | | | | | | |
| JUDR | | | | | | | | | | | | |
| JUDR | | | | | | | | | | | | |
| JUDR | | | | | | | | | | | | |
| JUDR | | | | | | | | | | | | |
| JUDR | | | | | | | | | | | | |
| JUDR | | | | | | | | | | | | |
| JUDR | | | | | | | | | | | | |
| JUDR | | | | | | | | | | | | |
| JUDR | | | | | | | | | | | | |
| JUDR | | | | | | | | | | | | |
| JUDR | | | | | | | | | | | | |

## VII. PROCEDURAL MOTIONS

TYPES:
- CCON – Another Case Consolidated with This One
- CHVN – Change of Venue
- CLAC – Class Actions
- INAP – Suggestion of Certification or for Interlocutory Appeal
- INTV – Intervention
- JOPT – Join Parties
- LFAM – Leave to File Amended Pleading
- MSPM – Miscellaneous Procedural Motions
- RMPT – Removal Petition
- SPCA – Sever Parties or Causes of Action
- STAY – Stay
- TRAD – Transferred from Another District
- TRAN – Transfer

CODES:
By: P1, P2, D1, D2, JD–Judge, MG–Magistrate
Versus: P1, P2, D1, D2, etc.
Brief: No. of Briefs
Special Discovery: Y–Yes or N–No
From: District Court Code

| TYPE | REF. NO. | MOTION | | | | | | DATE OF ORIGINAL COMPLAINT | NO. OF CASES CON-SOL. | DOCKET NOS. (2 Cases Maximum) | FROM TRAD | NO. OF PARTIES SEVERED OUT | NO. OF PARTIES ADDED | CLASS ACTIONS | | | | | DESCRIPTION AND COMMENTS |
| | | DATE | BY | VERSUS | R | ANSWER | | | | | | | | NOTICE OF CLASS DATE | SPEC DIS-COVERY | NOTICE MAILING DATE | SIZE OF CLASS | OPTING OUT DATE | |
| | | | | | | DATE | BRIEF | | | | | | | | | | | | |
| 6-9 | 10-11 | 13-17 | 18-19 INTV JOPT MSPM SPCA only | 20-21 INTV JOPT MSPM SPCA only | 22-23 INTV JOPT MSPM RMPT SPCA only | 24-28 INTV JOPT MSPM RMPT SPCA only | 30-31 INTV JOPT MSPM RMPT SPCA only | 32-37 RHPT | 38 CCON | 39-54 CCON | 55-58 TRAD | 59 SPCA | 60 JOPT | 61-66 | 67 | 68-73 | 74 | 75-80 | MSPM only |
| | | | | | | | | | | | | | | | | | | |
| | | | | | | | | | | | | | | | | | | |
| | | | | | | | | | | | | | | | | | | |
| | | | | | | | | | | | | | | | | | | |
| | | | | | | | | | | | | | | | | | | |
| | | | | | | | | | | | | | | | | | | |

VIII. CONTINUANCES

TYPES: CONT - Continuances of JUDR, PTCN, TRIL only
ENLG - Enlargements of time to answer motions, pleadings, discovery, and the discovery cutoff date
EXTN - Extension of time to file all motions, pleadings, and discovery

CODES: Movant: Pl, Dl, etc.
Action: G-Granted, D-Denied
By Whom: J-Judge, P-Parties, C-Clerk, U-Unknown
Subtype: C-Compel, O-Original, S-Sanctions

| TYPE | REF. NO. | CROSS REFERENCE | | | MOTION | | | RULING | | | ORIGINAL DATE SET | NEW DATE SET |
| | | TYPE | REF. NO. | SUBTYPE | DATE | MOVANT | ANSWER DATE | DATE | ACTION | BY WHOM | | |
| 8-9 | 10-11 | 12-15 | 16-17 | 18 | 19-24 | 25-26 | 27-32 | 33-38 | 39 | 40 | 41-46 | 47-52 |
| | | | | | | | | | | | | |
| | | | | | | | | | | | | |
| | | | | | | | | | | | | |
| | | | | | | | | | | | | |
| | | | | | | | | | | | | |
| | | | | | | | | | | | | |
| | | | | | | | | | | | | |

IX. TIMING CONTROLS

A. PRETRIAL CONFERENCE (PTCN)

CODES:
By: J-Judge, C-Clerk, M-Magistrate, O-Other
Length: L-Long, S-Short

| TYPE | REF. NO. | DISCOVERY CUTOFF | | | SCHEDULING PTCN | | | PRETRIAL CONFERENCE | | | PRETRIAL ORDER | |
| | | DATE | DATE SET FOR | BY | DATE OF SCHEDULING | DATE SET FOR | BY | DATE | NO. OF PARTIES ABSENT | BY | DATE | LENGTH OF DOCUMENTATION |
| 8-9 | 10-11 | 12-17 | 18-23 | 24 | 25-30 | 31-36 | 37 | 38-43 | 44-45 | 46 | 47-52 | 53-55 |
| PTCN | | | | | | | | | | | | |
| PTCN | | | | | | | | | | | | |
| PTCN | | | | | | | | | | | | |
| PTCN | | | | | | | | | | | | |
| PTCN | | | | | | | | | | | | |
| PTCN | | | | | | | | | | | | |
| PTCN | | | | | | | | | | | | |
| PTCN | | | | | | | | | | | | |

B. TRIAL

CODES:
Nonjury: Y-Yes, N-No
Pretrial Brief: Y-Yes, N-No
Under Advisement - Y-Yes, N-No

| TYPE | REF. NO. | SCHEDULING | | TRIAL | | | | UNDER ADVISEMENT | BRIEFING DATES | | OPINION RENDERED | |
| | | DATE OF SETTING | DATE SET FOR | DATE HELD | NO. OF DAYS | NONJURY | PRETRIAL BRIEFS | | PLAINTIFF | DEFENDANT | DATE | PAGES |
| 8-9 | 10-11 | 12-17 | 18-23 | 24-29 | 30-31 | 32 | 33 | 34 | 35-40 | 41-46 | 47-52 | 53-55 |
| TRIL | | | | | | | | | | | | |
| TRIL | | | | | | | | | | | | |
| TRIL | | | | | | | | | | | | |

CODES: Type: S-Settlement, T-Trial, M-Motion, F-Transfer, C-Consolidation, V-Voluntary Dismissal, O-Other
Prejudice: Y-Yes or N-No
Partial/Final: P or F

C. DISPOSITION

| TYPE | REF. NO. | DATE | DISP. TYPE | SETTLEMENT NOTICE DATE | PREJUDICE | PARTIAL/FINAL | NO. OF PARTIES OUT | EXECUTION OF JUDGEMENT DATE |
| 8-9 | 10-11 | 12-17 | 18 | 19-24 | 25 | 26 | 27-28 | 29-54 |
| DISP | | | | | | | | |
| DISP | | | | | | | | |
| DISP | | | | | | | | |
| DISP | | | | | | | | |

D. POST TRIAL

TYPES: AJPA - Motion to Arrest Judgment Pending Appeal
AMMJ - Motion to Amend Judgment or Relief from Judgment
MSPT - Miscellaneous Post Trial Motions
NTRI - Motion for New Trial

RCON - Motion to Reconsider

CODES: Filed by: Pl, Dl, JD-Judge, MG-Magistrate
Brief: 1-10
Subtype: C-Compel, O-Original, S-Sanctions

| TYPE | REF. NO. | CROSS REFERENCE | | | DATE | FILED BY | BRIEF | ANSWER | | DESCRIPTION |
| | | TYPE | REF. NO. | SUBTYPE | | | | DATE | BRIEF | MSPT only |
| 8-9 | 10-11 | 12-15 | 16-17 | 18 | 19-24 | 25-26 | 27-36 | 30-34 | 35-36 | |
| | | | | | | | | | | |
| | | | | | | | | | | |
| | | | | | | | | | | |

APPENDIX C

TELEPHONE SURVEY ON THE EXTENT OF FORMAL DISCOVERY

Because one of the objectives of this report was to systematically quantify discovery activity, it was important to determine the extent to which the collected data fairly represented all discovery requests and responses.

We were confident that discovery-related motion activity, which involves direct interaction between attorneys and the court, would be regularly recorded.

The extent of unrecorded request and response activity is known only by attorneys; therefore, we conducted a telephone survey of a sample of attorneys who had appeared in the cases under study. Only attorneys in private practice were sampled;[174] they were randomly selected from attorneys appearing in our case sample.[175] From their responses, we conclude that discovery reflected in the court records represents about three-fourths of discovery requests and responses in the cases under study.

Ten attorneys were called in each of the six metropolitan courts studied. The attorneys were not asked about particular cases that appeared in the sampled population; rather, they were asked about their general discovery-filing practices.

Table 43 is a summary of responses to the question: "[O]f the total number of requests for information you generally make in the typical civil

---

174. Pro se defendants; attorneys representing the United States, states and municipalities, legal aid groups, and the American Civil Liberties Union; and public defenders were not interviewed, primarily because it was expected that turnover in the staffs of these offices would have resulted in substantial numbers of nonresponses.

175. Any attorney, except those listed id., who represented a party in a case in the total case sample, was eligible for inclusion in the selected survey population. Each attorney was matched with a set of unique numbers reflecting the total number of parties represented. Since the attorney's office telephone number was used as the attorney identification code, this procedure accounted for both frequent appearances by a single attorney and appearances by several lawyers in a single law firm. Ten numbers were then selected at random, and an attorney (firm) was included in the survey if a selected number fell within the range of values assigned to the attorney (firm). A similar selection was then made, if necessary, to choose a single party from the list of parties represented by that attorney. If more than one selection number fell within a single attorney's range, a comparable number of parties was chosen from the list of clients. This party-selection step served to differentiate attorneys associated with a single firm. If a chosen attorney could not be contacted, a replacement was selected by repeating the above procedure, excluding previously selected attorneys.

federal case, what percentage do you file with the court?" The first column of the table shows the average percentage of filed requests reported by the attorneys in each of the courts studied. The second column shows the 95 percent confidence limits of these averages; that is, there was only one chance in twenty that another telephone survey would reveal an average percentage of formal discovery outside these ranges. For example, in the Southern District of Florida, there was only one chance in twenty that a new sample of attorneys appearing in the studied cases filed discovery at a rate outside of the range of 78.2 to 97.4 percent.

TABLE 43

PROPORTION OF DISCOVERY FILED BY ATTORNEYS

| Court | Average % Filed | 95% Confidence Interval of Averages |
|-------|-----------------|--------------------------------------|
| S.Fla. | 87.7 (2) | 78.2 - 97.4 |
| C.Cal. | 64.8 (5) | 43.2 - 86.4 |
| Md. | 74.5 (3) | 57.7 - 91.3 |
| E.La. | 56.0 (6) | 36.8 - 75.2 |
| E.Pa. | 72.5 (4) | 56.7 - 88.3 |
| Mass. | 88.0 (1) | 77.6 - 98.4 |
| Summary | 73.9 | 66.9 - 80.9 |

Note: Court ranks by average percentage of filed discovery are given in parentheses.

Table 43 shows that filing patterns differ substantially among the six courts. On the average, attorneys filed discovery most frequently in Massachusetts and Southern Florida, and least frequently in Eastern Louisiana.

Using this information, we estimated the total discovery activity per case in each court. Table 44 shows the results of this analysis. The average number of filed requests per discovered case is reported in the first column. The second column displays this average plus the amount of informal discovery revealed by the survey of attorneys. Again (because of the 95 percent confidence limits), we can be confident that only one time in twenty would the averages have fallen outside the ranges in column three.[176]

---

176. As an illustration, note that table 43 shows the Maryland attorneys responded that, on an average, 74.5% of their discovery was filed. To determine the total discovery activity of the Maryland attorneys, the average filed discovery requests per discovered case should be increased to account for the percentage of informal discovery. For Maryland, that meant an increase from 4.29 to 5.76 requests per discovered case. The range in table 43 of 57.7 to 91.3% provides 95% confidence that the average requests per case for the Maryland case sample was between 4.70 and 7.44 requests.

TABLE 44

RATE OF FORMAL AND INFORMAL DISCOVERY REQUESTS
PER DISCOVERED CASE
(Ranks in Parentheses)

| Court | Average Filed Discovery Requests per Discovered Case | | Average Total Discovery Requests per Discovered Case | | 95% Confidence Interval of Total Discovery |
|-------|-----|------|-----|------|--------------|
| S.Fla. | 5.51 | (1) | 6.28 | (4) | 5.66 - 7.05 |
| C.Cal. | 5.10 | (2) | 7.87 | (1) | 5.90 - 11.81 |
| Md. | 4.29 | (5) | 5.76 | (5) | 4.70 - 7.44 |
| E.La. | 3.79 | (6) | 6.77 | (3) | 5.04 - 10.30 |
| E.Pa. | 5.00 | (3) | 6.90 | (2) | 5.66 - 8.82 |
| Mass. | 4.62 | (4) | 5.25 | (6) | 4.70 - 5.95 |
| | | | | | |
| Summary | 4.74 | | 6.41 | | 5.86 - 7.09 |

Note: Total averages were derived by dividing the average filed discovery requests (table 44) by the average percentage filed (table 43). The confidence interval was derived by dividing the filed averages by the 95% confidence ranges given in table 43.

The most important conclusion to be drawn from the results of the telephone survey is that since it is very likely that between two-thirds and four-fifths of all discovery requests were filed with the court, the data in this report accurately reflect the actual discovery in the cases studied. But the data also lead to the important finding that total discovery activity does not vary widely between courts. In fact, since all the ranges in average total requests per court overlap, one cannot reject the possibility that there was no underlying difference between the courts. The difference between the highest and lowest average numbers of discovery requests is comparatively small for both the recorded data--1.72 requests (derived from table 44, column 1)--and for the requests adjusted to account for informal discovery--2.62 requests (derived from table 44, column 2).

Exhibit 1, the questionnaire used to conduct the survey, and tables 45 through 48, summarizing the attorneys' responses, are located following the text of this appendix. Not provided, however, are attorneys' explanations of differences in filing patterns between the courts. For example, the attorneys in Massachusetts stated that they frequently file discovery because in the state courts virtually all discovery was filed. In Southern Florida, another jurisdiction with a high filing rate, attorneys stated that they needed a "paper trail" to demonstrate to the federal judges that active discovery had been under way. This permitted an attorney faced with a discovery cutoff date to lay the foundation for a postponement. By contrast, in the Eastern District of Louisiana, which had a low filing rate, many of the attorneys indicated that because their specialty, admiralty practice, is a specialized area of law in which most practitioners have frequent professional contacts, they often sought discovery informally. Similar sentiments were expressed by the admiralty lawyers in Maryland and by lawyers specializing in intellectual property law (copyright, trademark, etc.) in Central California.

Attorneys also identified other factors as important considerations in deciding whether to file requests with the court. As indicated by table 48 (infra), more than half said that professional familiarity with opposing counsel, imposition of discovery cutoff dates, or the likelihood of trial would tend to result in filing discovery requests.

Table 47 (infra) shows the attorneys' patterns of filing with respect to different request types. For example, most attorneys stated that they "almost always" file interrogatories, deposition notices, and requests for admissions. Requests for documents, subpoenas duces tecum, and motions for physical and mental examinations were filed less often.

In conclusion, the fact that informal discovery undoubtedly does occur, and varies among districts, should be kept in mind in evaluating the data in this report, especially if the judge considers the rates of filings in setting discovery cutoff dates. But based on the results of the survey, we believe that the recorded data present a generally reliable indicator of the actual discovery in most cases. Variations disclosed in this survey, however, should be considered when interpreting recorded data.

## EXHIBIT 1

### ATTORNEY INTERVIEW QUESTIONNAIRE

I. Background Data

A. What percentage of your law practice is civil as opposed to criminal?

B. What percentage of your civil practice is in federal court as opposed to state court?

C. What percentage of your federal civil practice involves representing plaintiffs as opposed to defendants?

D. What percentage of your federal civil practice could be characterized as personal injury? Approximately what percentage of your federal civil practice is composed of other subject areas?

II. Overall Filing Practices

A. Directing your attention to discovery activity after the commencement of the action, of the total number of _requests_ for information you generally make in the typical federal civil case, what percentage do you file with the court?

B. Of the requests made to you after the commencement of the action, what percentage of your _responses_ do you file with the court?

III. Patterns for Individual Discovery Devices

Turning now to your filing practices for six specific types of discovery devices (interrogatories, oral depositions, document requests, requests for admissions, motions for mental and physical examinations, and subpoenas duces tecum), please indicate which of the following responses most closely characterizes your practice: almost always, usually, fifty-fifty, seldom, or almost never.

A. First, to what extent do you file your interrogatories with the court?

B. To what extent do you file notices of deposition?

C. When you seek admissions from parties, to what extent do you file the requests for admissions?

D. When you wish to inspect documents in the possession of parties, to what extent do you file document requests?

E. When you wish to inspect documents in the possession of nonparties, to what extent do you file a subpoena duces tecum?

F. When you seek mental or physical examinations of parties or witnesses, to what extent do you file a motion or any other notice?

G. When you respond to interrogatories you receive, to what extent do you file a response of any kind with the court?

H.  Of all the transcripts you order from oral depositions, to what extent do you file the transcripts?

I.  When you respond to requests for documents, to what extent do you file a response, such as a notice of furnishing documents, copies of the documents themselves, or objections?

J.  Of all the responses you make to requests for admissions, to what extent do you file your objections, denials, or admissions with the court?

IV.  Factors Influencing Filing Patterns

First, what are the significant factors you generally take into account in deciding whether to file a _request_ for discovery with the court?  Which of the following factors play an important role in your decision?

A.  Professional familiarity with an opposing attorney

B.  The amount in controversy

C.  The importance of the subject matter of the litigation

D.  The approach of a termination date for discovery

E.  The substantial likelihood of trial

F.  Are the factors that influence your decision whether or not to file _responses_ any different from the factors that influence your decision to file requests?

G.  Would the service of a request for discovery information on you be a factor in your decision to file that response with the court?

H.  In your opinion, do the answers you gave to the questionnaire reflect the general discovery practices of the other federal practitioners in your district?

## TABLE 45

ATTORNEY SURVEY SUMMARY STATISTICS:
PROFESSIONAL BACKGROUND
(Average Responses)

| I. Background Data | S.Fla. | C.Cal. | Md. | E.La. | E.Pa. | Mass. | All Courts |
|---|---|---|---|---|---|---|---|
| A. Percentage of civil practice | 100 | 97 | 95 | 97 | 96 | 98 | 97 |
| B. Percentage of federal practice | 56 | 61 | 47 | 73 | 72 | 55 | 61 |
| C. Percentage representing plaintiff | 52 | 56 | 37 | 57 | 45 | 48 | 49 |
| D. Percentage of personal injury[a] | 1 | 0 | 37 | 41 | 34 | 47 | 27 |

[a]Other types of practice were too diverse to summarize in this table.

## TABLE 46

ATTORNEY SURVEY SUMMARY STATISTICS:
FILING PRACTICES
(Average Responses)

| II. Overall Filing Practices | S.Fla. | C.Cal. | Md. | E.La. | E.Pa. | Mass. | All Courts |
|---|---|---|---|---|---|---|---|
| A. Percentage of requests filed | 88 | 64 | 75 | 56 | 72 | 88 | 74 |
| B. Percentage of responses filed | 86 | 71 | 81 | 50 | 72 | 84 | 74 |

TABLE 47

ATTORNEY SURVEY SUMMARY STATISTICS:
FREQUENCY OF FILING SPECIFIC DISCOVERY DEVICES
(Average Responses)

|  | S.Fla. | C.Cal. | Md. | E.La. | E.Pa. | Mass. | All Courts |
|---|---|---|---|---|---|---|---|
| III. Patterns for Individual Discovery Devices | | | | | | | |
| **A. Requests for interrogatories** | | | | | | | |
| Almost always | 7 | 7 | 10 | 7 | 8 | 10 | 49 |
| Usually | 0 | 0 | 0 | 2 | 0 | 0 | 2 |
| 50-50 | 2 | 1 | 0 | 0 | 0 | 0 | 3 |
| Seldom | 1 | 1 | 0 | 1 | 0 | 0 | 3 |
| Almost never | 0 | 1 | 0 | 0 | 2 | 0 | 3 |
| No response | 0 | 0 | 0 | 0 | 0 | 0 | 0 |
| **B. Notices of deposition** | | | | | | | |
| Almost always | 8 | 3 | 9 | 3 | 6 | 10 | 39 |
| Usually | 0 | 3 | 0 | 4 | 0 | 0 | 7 |
| 50-50 | 1 | 2 | 0 | 2 | 1 | 0 | 6 |
| Seldom | 1 | 1 | 1 | 1 | 2 | 0 | 6 |
| Almost never | 0 | 1 | 0 | 0 | 0 | 0 | 1 |
| No response | 0 | 0 | 0 | 0 | 1 | 0 | 1 |
| **C. Requests for admissions** | | | | | | | |
| Almost always | 8 | 6 | 8 | 6 | 10 | 9 | 47 |
| Usually | 0 | 1 | 1 | 1 | 0 | 1 | 4 |
| 50-50 | 1 | 1 | 1 | 3 | 0 | 0 | 6 |
| Seldom | 0 | 1 | 0 | 0 | 0 | 0 | 1 |
| Almost never | 0 | 1 | 0 | 0 | 0 | 0 | 1 |
| No response | 1 | 0 | 0 | 0 | 0 | 0 | 1 |
| **D. Document requests** | | | | | | | |
| Almost always | 5 | 1 | 5 | 1 | 4 | 8 | 24 |
| Usually | 2 | 3 | 2 | 4 | 2 | 1 | 14 |
| 50-50 | 1 | 3 | 1 | 3 | 3 | 0 | 11 |
| Seldom | 2 | 2 | 2 | 2 | 0 | 0 | 8 |
| Almost never | 0 | 1 | 0 | 0 | 1 | 1 | 3 |
| No response | 0 | 0 | 0 | 0 | 0 | 0 | 0 |
| **E. Subpoenas duces tecum** | | | | | | | |
| Almost always | 9 | 5 | 3 | 3 | 5 | 3 | 28 |
| Usually | 0 | 1 | 4 | 3 | 1 | 3 | 12 |
| 50-50 | 0 | 0 | 2 | 2 | 2 | 2 | 8 |
| Seldom | 1 | 3 | 0 | 2 | 0 | 1 | 7 |
| Almost never | 0 | 1 | 0 | 0 | 0 | 1 | 2 |
| No response | 0 | 0 | 1 | 0 | 2 | 0 | 3 |

TABLE 47--Continued

F. Physical
   or mental
   examinations

| | | | | | | |
|---|---|---|---|---|---|---|
| Almost always | 1 | 0 | 1 | 0 | 0 | 3 | 5 |
| Usually | 0 | 0 | 0 | 1 | 1 | 0 | 2 |
| 50-50 | 3 | 0 | 1 | 1 | 0 | 5 | 10 |
| Seldom | 0 | 0 | 1 | 6 | 4 | 0 | 11 |
| Almost never | 0 | 2 | 3 | 1 | 2 | 1 | 9 |
| No response | 6 | 8 | 4 | 1 | 3 | 1 | 23 |

G. Answers to
   interrogatories

| | | | | | | |
|---|---|---|---|---|---|---|
| Almost always | 10 | 9 | 10 | 8 | 8 | 9 | 54 |
| Usually | 0 | 0 | 0 | 1 | 0 | 0 | 1 |
| 50-50 | 0 | 0 | 0 | 1 | 1 | 1 | 3 |
| Seldom | 0 | 0 | 0 | 0 | 0 | 0 | 0 |
| Almost never | 0 | 1 | 0 | 0 | 1 | 0 | 2 |
| No response | 0 | 0 | 0 | 0 | 0 | 0 | 0 |

H. Deposition
   transcripts

| | | | | | | |
|---|---|---|---|---|---|---|
| Almost always | 10 | 0 | 2 | 6 | 1 | 0 | 19 |
| Usually | 0 | 3 | 1 | 2 | 1 | 0 | 7 |
| 50-50 | 0 | 2 | 1 | 1 | 1 | 0 | 5 |
| Seldom | 0 | 3 | 6 | 0 | 3 | 5 | 17 |
| Almost never | 0 | 1 | 0 | 0 | 3 | 5 | 9 |
| No response | 0 | 1 | 0 | 1 | 1 | 0 | 3 |

I. Production
   of documents

| | | | | | | |
|---|---|---|---|---|---|---|
| Almost always | 6 | 6 | 5 | 1 | 1 | 3 | 22 |
| Usually | 3 | 0 | 2 | 2 | 0 | 2 | 9 |
| 50-50 | 1 | 2 | 0 | 2 | 2 | 1 | 8 |
| Seldom | 0 | 0 | 2 | 5 | 6 | 3 | 16 |
| Almost never | 0 | 1 | 1 | 0 | 1 | 1 | 4 |
| No response | 0 | 1 | 0 | 0 | 0 | 0 | 1 |

J. Responses to
   requests for
   admissions

| | | | | | | |
|---|---|---|---|---|---|---|
| Almost always | 9 | 7 | 10 | 7 | 8 | 9 | 50 |
| Usually | 1 | 1 | 0 | 2 | 0 | 0 | 4 |
| 50-50 | 0 | 0 | 0 | 1 | 0 | 0 | 1 |
| Seldom | 0 | 1 | 0 | 0 | 1 | 1 | 3 |
| Almost never | 0 | 1 | 0 | 0 | 0 | 0 | 1 |
| No response | 0 | 0 | 0 | 0 | 1 | 0 | 1 |

## TABLE 48

### ATTORNEY SURVEY SUMMARY STATISTICS:
### FACTORS THAT INFLUENCE DECISIONS TO FILE DISCOVERY
### (Average Responses)

| IV. Factors Influencing Filing Patterns[a] | S.Fla. | C.Cal. | Md. | E.La. | E.Pa. | Mass. | Summary |
|---|---|---|---|---|---|---|---|
| A. Professional familiarity | | | | | | | |
| % Yes | 50 | 80 | 70 | 90 | 80 | 30 | 67 |
| B. Amount in controversy | | | | | | | |
| % Yes | 30 | 70 | 60 | 60 | 20 | 40 | 43 |
| C. Subject matter | | | | | | | |
| % Yes | 40 | 50 | 44 | 40 | 40 | 30 | 41 |
| D. Cutoff date | | | | | | | |
| % Yes | 60 | 67 | 60 | 80 | 78 | 60 | 68 |
| E. Likelihood of trial | | | | | | | |
| % Yes | 50 | 40 | 67 | 90 | 80 | 50 | 63 |
| F. Different factors considered for responses than for requests | | | | | | | |
| % Yes | 10 | 0 | 10 | 20 | 30 | 25 | 16 |
| G. Service of a request | | | | | | | |
| % Yes | 50 | 75 | 100 | 100 | 90 | 100 | 86 |
| H. Do your answers reflect district practices? | | | | | | | |
| % Yes | 86 | 57 | 83 | 75 | 80 | 88 | 78 |

[a] An open-ended question in this section asked about the factors influencing filing patterns (see exhibit 1), but the responses to this question were not reported because this information does not differ significantly from the responses to the specific questions asked.

APPENDIX D

## PROTECTING MOTIONS

The federal rules provide a variety of mechanisms for resolving discovery disputes. Chapter three examines the effectiveness of mechanisms available to requesting parties: the compelling and sanction provisions of rule 37. The discovery rules also provide requested parties with the right to block a request for discovery if the request is intended to harass the requested party.[177] We call these protecting motions; they include motions to quash (rule 45(b)), motions for protective orders (rule 26(c)), and motions to terminate or limit depositions (rule 30(d)).

In examining protecting motions, we could not compare the number of motions to "eligible" events. As with the sanction provisions of rule 37, the rule provisions for protecting motions turn on events not recorded in the court files--primarily annoying, embarrassing, or oppressive requests; unduly burdensome or expensive requests; or bad faith by the requesting party. We have no data to measure the extent of such conduct by requesting parties. Consequently, we could not measure the actual protecting motions against those that might have been sought, nor could we measure the number of protecting motions that were frivolously sought.

Nonetheless, we studied recorded protecting motions (see table 49) to determine whether the level of activity was extensive enough to indicate substantial overreaching in discovery by requesting parties or substantial use of protecting motions by requested parties to delay a requirement to respond.

To conclude that protecting motions are abused in either of these ways by attorneys, we would have to find that protecting motions were brought fairly frequently. In that case, judicial responses would suggest whether it was requesting or requested parties who were abusing the process: a high percentage of grantings would indicate that requesting parties are frequently overreaching; a high percentage of denials would indicate that requested parties are seeking to delay legitimate responses.

The data in table 49 show that requested parties seldom resort to protecting motions, indicating no pervasive use of the protecting provisions of the rules to delay discovery. The 56.9 percent granting rate also indicates that these motions more often than not have a basis in fact.

---

177. A requested party may also object to a request, and thereby shift the burden to the requesting party to file a compelling motion.

105

## TABLE 49

### NUMBER OF PROTECTING MOTIONS, RULINGS, AND GRANTINGS

| Types of Protecting Motions (Events) | No. Events | Protecting Motions per Event (Total Motions) | No. Rulings (% Motions) | No. Grantings (% Rulings) |
|---|---|---|---|---|
| Motions to quash (subpoena duces tecum, written questions of witnesses, notices to depose witnesses and custodians) | 888 | 1 in 27 (33) | 17 (51.5%) | 7 (41.2%) |
| Motions for protective orders | | | | |
| (Notices of deposition of parties, doctors, experts, witnesses) | 2,832 | 1 in 18 (156) | 94 (50.2%) | 55 (58.5%) |
| Motions to limit or terminate depositions | | | | |
| (Holding of depositions of parties or witnesses) | 568 | 1 in 33 (20) | 12 (60.2%) | 8 (56.7%) |
| Summary | 4,388 | 1 in 21 (209) | 123 (58.9%) | 70· (56.9%) |

The infrequency of protecting motions suggests alternative inferences about overreaching by requesting parties:

1.  Requesting parties do not often harass in using their rights to obtain discovery, or

2.  Requesting parties often harass in using requests, but requested parties seldom use protecting motions to constrain these abuses.

Based on these data, we cannot say which inference is more reasonable. We know that certain factors would restrict the use of protecting motions notwithstanding possible abuses by requesting parties. For one, the present rule provisions governing the use of protecting motions are quite narrow; for another, the "broad liberal treatment" to be accorded the discovery rules under Hickman v. Taylor[178] may deter expansive judicial interpretations of the protecting provisions.

---

178.  329 U.S. 495 (1947).

Finally, there is support for the view that judges generally accord great deference to the liberality of the discovery rules. Though rulings on protecting motions tend to favor the moving party, the tendency is not nearly so strong as that in rulings on compelling motions directed to substance.[179] Judges are shown to overwhelmingly permit requesting parties to compel discovery, but are far less likely to permit requested parties to block discovery.

TABLE 50

NUMBER OF SUBSTANTIVE COMPELLING MOTIONS,
RULINGS, AND GRANTINGS
BY REQUEST TYPE

| Request Type | No. Requests | Compelling Motions per Request (Total Motions) | No. Rulings (% Motions) | No. Grantings (% Rulings) |
|---|---|---|---|---|
| Interrogatories | 1,714 | 1 in 13 (135) | 84 (62.2%) | 76 (90.5%) |
| Requests for documents | 310 | 1 in 7 (42) | 30 (71.4%) | 29 (96.7%) |
| Summary | 2,024 | 1 in 11 (177) | 114 (64.4%) | 105 (92.1%) |

---

179. Compare table 6 (analyzing compelling motions on tardiness grounds).

ANALYSIS OF DISCOVERY USE BY CASE TYPE

LEGEND FOR CASE TYPE CATEGORIES

**Admn. law (1-10)**
1 Freedom of Information Act
2 Agency appeals
3 Social Security
4 Other
5 Social Security - black lung
6 Coal Mine and Safety Act civil penalty

**Admiralty (11-20)**
11 Collision
12 Cargo damage
13 Service, repair and wage claims
14 Contracts (mortgage, charter, etc.)
15 Tort (nonpersonal)
16 Penalty
17 Other
18 Cargo loss

**Bankruptcy Appeals**
21 Corporate
22 Individual
23 Other
24 Setting aside voidable transfers if bankruptcy already adjudicated

**Civil rights (31-40) private plaintiff**
31 42 U.S.C. § 1983, et seq.
32 Injunction versus state law (3-judge court)
33 All other types of discrimination

**govt. plaintiff**
35 EEOC
36 Civil Service
37 Civil Rights Commission
38 Other

**Constitutional law (41-50)**
41 General

**Contracts (51-65)**
51 Realty
52 Warranty
53 Promissory note
54 Simple (two-party only)
55 Construction
56 Employment
57 Suretyship (Miller Act, SBA and FHA loans)
58 Franchise
59 Government
60 Securities (including fraud and 10b-5)
61 Transportation
62 Insurance
63 Services
64 Other

**Environmental law (66-70)**
66 General

**Fed. statutory actions (71-80)**
71 Food and Drug Act
72 HUD and Housing Act
73 Garnishment of federal employees
74 Truth-in-Lending
75 OSHA
76 Seizure
77 Other

**ICC (81-90)**
81 Penalty
82 Cargo damage
83 Tariff and charges

Intellectual prop. (91-100)
91 Copyrights
92 Patents
93 Trademarks

Labor (101-110)
101 Injunctions
102 Unfair labor practices (civil)
103 Hours and wages
104 Collective bargaining
105 Labor-Management Reporting and Disclosure Act
106 Discriminatory hiring
107 Other

Military
111 General (including wrongful dismissal)

N.A.R.A. (121-130)
121 Civil commitments for treatment

Naturalization (131-140)
131 Deportation
132 Other appeals

Prisoner pet.
141 Federal
142 State

143 Federal
144 State

Real property (151-155)
151 Federal condemnation
152 State condemnation
153 Ejectment
154 Other

Seizures (156-160)
156 Food and Drug Act (spoilage)
157 Contraband (drugs, stolen goods, etc.)
158 Tax deficiency, attachment
159 Obscene materials (Postal Service)

Tax (161-170)
163 Penalty
164 Estate
165 Corporate
166 Partnership
167 Individual proprietorship
168 Personal
169 Other

Tort (171-190)

statutory
171 F.E.L.A.
172 Federal Tort Claims Act
173 Jones Act (seaman injuries)
174 Other federal statutes

diversity
175 Product liability
176 Slip and fall
177 Marine (nonseaman, personal injury)
178 Auto
179 Other
180 Fraud (other than securities and bankruptcy)
181 Actual damages
182 Libel, abuse of process, slander
183 Consequential damages
184 Airlines
185 Legal and medical malpractice
186 Miscellaneous

LEGEND FOR CASE TYPE CATEGORIES--Continued

Trade reg.
(191-200)
govt.
plaintiff

private
plaintiff

191   Justice Department
192   FTC

193   Price fixing
194   Monopoly
195   Robinson-Patman Act
196   Unfair competition (not
         trademarks)
197   Other (auto dealer's
         day-in-court)

Other       201

## TABLE 51

### ANALYSIS OF DISCOVERY USE BY CASE TYPE
(Cumulative Percentages)

| Request Categories | 31+ | | 21-30 | | 11-20 | | 3-10 | | 1-2 | | 0 | | Total Cases |
|---|---|---|---|---|---|---|---|---|---|---|---|---|---|
| | No. | % | No. | % | No. | % | No. | % | No. | % | No. | % | |
| **Area of Litigation** Case Type Code[a] | | | | | | | | | | | | | |
| Admn. law   2 | | | | | | | 1 | (3.7) | 2 | (11.1) | 24 | (100) | 27 |
| 3 | | | | | | | | | 2 | (5.3) | 36 | (100) | 38 |
| 4 | | | | | | | | | | | 2 | (100) | 2 |
| 9 | | | | | | | | | | | 1 | (100) | 1 |
| Admiralty   11 | 1 | (1.4) | 3 | (5.8) | 2 | (8.7) | 17 | (33.3) | 20 | (62.3) | 26 | (100) | 69 |
| 12 | | | | | 3 | (2.3) | 1 | (16.3) | 39 | (46.5) | 69 | (100) | 129 |
| 13 | | | | | 2 | (3.8) | 8 | (19.2) | 9 | (36.5) | 33 | (100) | 52 |
| 14 | | | | | 2 | (5.1) | 8 | (26.3) | 7 | (44.7) | 21 | (100) | 38 |
| 15 | | | | | 1 | (9.1) | 7 | (72.7) | | | 3 | (100) | 11 |
| 16 | | | | | | | | | | | 5 | (100) | 5 |

| | | | | | | | |
|---|---|---|---|---|---|---|---|
| 17 | | | | | 3 (50.0) | 3 (100) | 6 |
| 18 | | | | 1 (100) | | | 1 |
| 21 | Bankruptcy appeals | | | | 2 (66.7) | 1 (100) | 3 |
| 24 | | | | 3 (18.8) | 3 (37.5) | 10 (100) | 16 |
| 31 | Civil rights private plaintiff | | 1 (1.1) | 13 (15.6) | 27 (45.6) | 49 (100) | 90 |
| 32 | | | | 1 (10.0) | 2 (30.0) | 7 (100) | 10 |
| 33 | | 1 (1.7) | 1 (3.3) | 13 (25.0) | 14 (48.3) | 31 (100) | 60 |
| 35 | govt. plaintiff | | | 1 (11.1) | 1 (22.2) | 7 (100) | 9 |
| 37 | | | | | 1 (100) | | 1 |
| 38 | | | | 1 (50.0) | 1 (100) | | 2 |
| 41 | Constitu- tional law | | 1 (3.2) | 3 (12.9) | 5 (29.0) | 22 (100) | 31 |
| 47 | | | | | | 1 (100) | 1 |
| 51 | Contracts | | 3 (9.7) | 12 (48.4) | 6 (67.7) | 10 (100) | 31 |
| 52 | | | 4 (16.0) | 10 (56.0) | 4 (72.0) | 7 (100) | 25 |

TABLE 51--Continued

| Request Categories<br>Area of Litigation<br>Case Type Code[a] | 31+<br>No. | % | 21-30<br>No. | % | 11-20<br>No. | % | 3-10<br>No. | % | 1-2<br>No. | % | 0<br>No. | % | Total<br>Cases |
|---|---|---|---|---|---|---|---|---|---|---|---|---|---|
| 53 | | | | | 2 | (4.0) | 12 | (28.0) | 7 | (42.0) | 29 | (100) | 50 |
| 54 | 1 | (0.8) | | | 1 | (1.7) | 33 | (28.1) | 30 | (52.9) | 56 | (100) | 121 |
| 55 | | | | | 1 | (2.7) | 8 | (24.3) | 8 | (45.9) | 20 | (100) | 37 |
| 56 | | | | | | | 15 | (38.5) | 7 | (56.4) | 17 | (100) | 39 |
| 57 | | | | | | | 7 | (18.4) | 5 | (31.6) | 26 | (100) | 38 |
| 58 | | | | | 6 | (26.1) | 6 | (52.2) | 4 | (69.6) | 7 | (100) | 23 |
| 59 | | | | | | | 4 | (40.0) | 1 | (50.0) | 5 | (100) | 10 |
| 60 | 2 | (2.3) | 1 | (3.5) | 7 | (11.5) | 36 | (52.9) | 15 | (70.1) | 26 | (100) | 87 |
| 61 | | | | | | | 2 | (25.0) | 2 | (50.0) | 4 | (100) | 8 |
| 62 | | | | | 1 | (1.4) | 24 | (35.2) | 15 | (56.3) | 31 | (100) | 71 |
| 63 | | | | | | | 5 | (31.3) | 3 | (50.0) | 8 | (100) | 16 |

| | | | | | |
|---|---|---|---|---|---|
| | 64 | | 1 (25.0) | 1 (7.7) | 12 (100) | 13 |
| | 65 | 1 (100) | | 1 (50.0) | 2 (100) | 4 |
| Environmental law | 66 | 1 (100) | | | | 1 |
| Fed. statutory actions | 71 | | | | 3 (100) | 3 |
| | 72 | | 1 (25.0) | | 3 (100) | 4 |
| | 73 | | 1 (100) | | | 1 |
| | 74 | 3 (13.0) | 10 (56.5) | | 10 (100) | 23 |
| | 75 | | | | 8 (100) | 8 |
| | 76 | 1 (14.3) | 1 (28.6) | | 5 (100) | 7 |
| | 77 | 2 (7.4) | 5 (25.9) | | 20 (100) | 27 |
| | 78 | | | | 1 (100) | 1 |
| ICC | 81 | | 3 (27.3) | | 8 (100) | 11 |
| | 82 | 1 (7.7) | 2 (23.1) | 4 (53.8) | 6 (100) | 13 |
| | 83 | | 2 (8.3) | | 22 (100) | 24 |

TABLE 51--Continued

| Request Categories Case Type Code | 31+ No. | % | 21-30 No. | % | 11-20 No. | % | 3-10 No. | % | 1-2 No. | % | 0 No. | % | Total Cases |
|---|---|---|---|---|---|---|---|---|---|---|---|---|---|
| **Area of Litigation** | | | | | | | | | | | | | |
| Intellectual prop. | | | | | | | | | | | | | |
| 91 | | | | | | | 7 | (22.6) | 8 | (48.4) | 16 | (100) | 31 |
| 92 | 1 | (2.9) | 3 | (11.8) | 4 | (26.5) | 7 | (47.1) | 12 | (82.4) | 6 | (100) | 34 |
| 93 | | | 2 | (4.9) | 1 | (7.3) | 10 | (31.7) | 11 | (58.5) | 17 | (100) | 41 |
| Labor | | | | | | | | | | | | | |
| 101 | | | | | | | | | 1 | (20.0) | 4 | (100) | 5 |
| 102 | | | 1 | (3.1) | | | 6 | (21.9) | 6 | (4C.6) | 19 | (100) | 32 |
| 103 | | | | | 1 | (3.1) | 5 | (18.8) | 9 | (46.9) | 17 | (100) | 32 |
| 104 | | | | | | | 21 | (21.2) | 38 | (59.6) | 40 | (100) | 99 |
| 105 | | | | | | | 2 | (28.6) | | | 5 | (100) | 7 |
| 106 | | | | | | | | | 3 | (100) | | | 3 |

| Code | Category | | | | | Total |
|---|---|---|---|---|---|---|
| 107 | | | | | 4 (100) | 4 |
| 111 | Military | | 1 (6.3) | 2 (18.8) | 13 (100) | 16 |
| 121 | N.A.R.A. | | | 1 | 1 (100) | 1 |
| 131 | Naturalization | | | 1 (12.5) | 7 (100) | 8 |
| 132 | | | | 8 | 8 (100) | 8 |
| 141 | Prisoner pet. habeas | | | 1 (1.6) | 60 (100) | 61 |
| 142 | | | | 6 (2.2) | 273 (100) | 279 |
| 143 | Prisoner pet. civil rights | 1 (2.5) | 3 (25.0) | 9 (100) | 12 |
| 144 | | 1 (1.2) | 7 (11.1) | 3 (14.8) | 69 (100) | 81 |
| 151 | Real property | | 3 (8.8) | 5 (23.5) | 26 (100) | 34 |
| 152 | | | | 1 | 1 (100) | 1 |
| 153 | | | | 3 | 3 (100) | 3 |

TABLE 51--Continued

| Request Categories<br>Case Type Code[a] | 31+ | | 21-30 | | 11-20 | | 3-10 | | 1-2 | | 0 | | Total Cases |
|---|---|---|---|---|---|---|---|---|---|---|---|---|---|
| | No. | % | No. | % | No. | % | No. | % | No. | % | No. | % | |
| **Area of Litigation** | | | | | | | | | | | | | |
| Seizures | | | | | | | | | | | | | |
| 154 | | | | | | | | | | | 3 | (100) | 3 |
| 156 | | | | | | | | | | | 13 | (100) | 13 |
| 157 | | | | | | | 1 | (7.1) | 2 | (14.3) | 12 | (100) | 14 |
| 158 | | | | | 1 | (20.0) | | | 1 | (40.0) | 3 | (100) | 5 |
| 159 | | | | | | | | | | | 6 | (100) | 6 |
| Tax | | | | | | | | | | | | | |
| 161 | | | | | | | | | | | 1 | (100) | 1 |
| 162 | | | | | | | | | | | 5 | (100) | 5 |
| 163 | | | | | | | | | 1 | (50.0) | 1 | (100) | 2 |
| 164 | | | | | | | | | 3 | (100) | | | 3 |
| 165 | | | | | | | 3 | (42.9) | 2 | (71.4) | 2 | (100) | 7 |
| 167 | | | | | | | | | | | 2 | (100) | 2 |

| | C1 | C2 | C3 | C4 | C5 | C6 | Total |
|---|---|---|---|---|---|---|---|
| 168 | | | | 9 (27.3) | 6 (45.5) | 1 (100) | 33 |
| 169 | | | | | | 2 (100) | 2 |
| 171 Tort statutory | | 1 (1.4) | 2 (4.2) | 30 (46.5) | 29 (87.3) | 9 (100) | 71 |
| 172 | | | 2 (4.7) | 9 (25.6) | 13 (55.8) | 19 (100) | 43 |
| 173 | 1 (0.4) | 3 (1.4) | 32 (13.0) | 109 (52.3) | 80 (81.2) | 52 (100) | 277 |
| 174 | | | | | | 1 (100) | 1 |
| 175 | 6 (1.0) | 2 (13.3) | 9 (28.3) | 22 (65.0) | 13 (86.7) | 8 (100) | 60 |
| 176 | | | 3 (11.1) | 13 (59.3) | 6 (81.5) | 5 (100) | 27 |
| 177 diversity | | | 1 (7.1) | 5 (42.9) | 5 (78.6) | 3 (100) | 14 |
| 178 | | | 3 (1.7) | 86 (50.9) | 50 (79.4) | 36 (100) | 175 |
| 180 | | | 1 (8.3) | 2 (25.0) | 1 (33.3) | 8 (100) | 12 |
| 182 | | 1 (7.1) | | 3 (28.6) | 4 (57.1) | 6 (100) | 14 |
| 184 | | 1 (4.0) | 2 (12.0) | 6 (36.0) | 8 (68.0) | 8 (100) | 25 |
| 185 | | | 2 (15.4) | 6 (61.5) | 1 (69.2) | 4 (100) | 13 |

TABLE 51--Continued

| Request Categories / Case Type Code[a] | 31+ No. | % | 21-30 No. | % | 11-20 No. | % | 3-10 No. | % | 1-2 No. | % | 0 No. | % | Total Cases |
|---|---|---|---|---|---|---|---|---|---|---|---|---|---|
| Area of Litigation | | | | | | | | | | | | | |
| Tort miscellaneous   186 | | | 1 | (1.4) | 8 | (13.0) | 28 | (53.6) | 16 | (76.8) | 16 | (100) | 69 |
| Trade reg. govt. plaintiff   191 | | | | | | | 1 | (100) | | | | | 1 |
| 192 | | | | | | | | | 1 | (100) | | | 1 |
| 193 | | | 1 | (5.3) | 1 | (10.5) | 10 | (63.2) | 4 | (84.2) | 3 | (100) | 19 |
| 194 | | | | | | | 3 | (27.3) | 2 | (45.5) | 6 | (100) | 11 |
| private plaintiff   195 | | | | | 3 | (42.9) | 1 | (57.1) | 1 | (71.4) | 2 | (100) | 7 |
| 196 | | | | | 1 | (9.1) | 5 | (54.5) | 1 | (63.6) | 4 | (100) | 11 |
| Other   201 | | | | | 1 | (1.3) | 7 | (10.6) | 10 | (24.0) | 57 | (100) | 75 |

[a]There are 108 case type categories; five of them had no cases in the sample.

## APPENDIX F

### CLUSTERING AND BALANCING
#### Clustering

As described in chapter five, a single case can be considered to be tightly clustered to the extent that its discovery requests are filed at approximately the same time; a case is loosely clustered if its discovery requests are spread out evenly. This conceptual definition can be made operational in the following way. If a case has two or fewer requests, there cannot be clustering, since it takes two events to define the discovery period itself, and a third request is needed for the notion of clustering to be defined.

However, with three or more requests, clustering can be a fairly rich measure. The notion of the "total discovery period"--the maximum interval between requests--is basic here. This is the time from the filing date of the first request to the date of the last request, whether it be five days or five hundred days, as long as it is one day or more. If all requests are filed on the same day, measurement of clustering is not possible.

The simplest example of clustering is a case in which there are three requests. If two of them are filed on the same day, the case is maximally clustered, since it does not matter whether that day is at the beginning of the discovery period or the end. In fact, there are two intervals here: from one request of a simultaneous pair to the other (0 days), and from either to the last request (N days). (If there are M requests, and M is greater than 1, there are M-1 intervals). Minimal clustering with three requests occurs when one is filed exactly between the other two; the intervals are the same length. The average interval, with three requests, is N/2 days, where N is the total discovery period. (With M requests, the average interval is N/(M-1) days.) The next step is determining the extent to which a particular interval differs from the average. If most intervals are close to the average, they are very loosely clustered; if they differ widely from the average, they are tightly clustered. In the three-request case, the maximally clustered situation is two intervals, of 0 and N days, and the minimally clustered situation is two intervals, both of which are N/2 days. Both of the latter intervals are equal to the average; both of the former are N/2 days away. One can then characterize an entire case by determining the extent to which each interval differs from the average interval:

$$\text{Abs-score} = \frac{\sum_{i=1}^{M} |Int_i - \overline{Int}|}{N}$$

where

$Int_i$ = Size of the ith interval

$\overline{Int}$ = Size of average interval

M = Number of intervals

N = Total discovery period

Moreover, the maximum difference (the sum of the absolute differences between each interval and the average interval) can be expressed as:

$$\text{Max} = \frac{2 \times N \times (M - 1)}{M^2}$$

where

Max = Maximum clustering possible, given M and N.

Calculating the maximum possible clustering score permits comparing the extent of clustering between cases with different M's and N's. Knowing the maximum permits us to calculate a relative clustering score by dividing a particular case's actual score by its possible maximum:

$$\text{Rel-score} = \frac{\text{Abs-score}}{\text{Max}}$$

All cases' relative scores will then vary from 0 (no clustering, evenly divided along the total discovery period) to 1 (maximal clustering, all requests except one filed at the same time). This number, then, is the clustering score used in the analysis.

## Balancing

The intuitive notion of balance in a case is similar to a child's seesaw: the balance point is where one would put the fulcrum to balance the heavy child and the lighter one. If both are the same weight, the fulcrum goes in the middle; if one weighs twice the other, the fulcrum should be two-thirds of the way towards the heavier one.

The seesaw represents the total length of the discovery period, from the first request to the last. If most of the time intervals are towards the beginning of the period, the weight of the process is "on the left," and the balance point is closer to the left (beginning). If there is as much time on the left as on the right, then the balance is in the middle. Similarly, if most of the time is towards the end, the balance is towards the "right."

Conceptually, the balance is the point at which half the discovery activity occurs before it, and half after it. It is calculated by subtracting the time of the first discovery request from the time of each other request, adding those values for all requests (except the first, which is 0, and the last, which is N) and dividing by N (the time of the total discovery period).

If all requests (except the last) are filed at the same time as the first, the value for the balance is 0. If all requests (except the first) are filed at the same time as the last, the value is 1. Any other possibilities have values between 0 and 1, with 0.5 indicating an even "balance.

## DISCOVERY BY TYPE OF CASE TERMINATION

Variation in the use of discovery for cases with different types of disposition discloses variation in the potential contribution of discovery. There are four major types of termination: voluntary dismissal, motion, settlement, and trial.

We expected that voluntary dismissal would usually occur without discovery. Trials were expected to be preceded by discovery in nearly all cases. Expectations about discovery activity in cases terminated by motion and settlement were less firm. Frequency of discovery by type of disposition is shown in figure 8.

As expected, voluntary dismissals usually occurred without discovery, and discovery preceded most trials. The fact that some trials were held without recorded discovery was not surprising, since informal methods may have been sufficient.[180]

A substantial percentage of the settled cases had no discovery exchanges. Apparently, parties can often settle their differences without resorting to discovery. However, discovery could well have contributed to nearly two-thirds of the settlements in the sample. Only one-third of the motion-terminated cases involved discovery.

Figure 9 shows the variation in discovered cases for eight motion types.[181] Among the four most frequent types, the variations are substantial but not surprising. Default and rule 12 motions commonly occur before joinder of issue when discovery has not begun. Summary judgment[182] and dismissal for failure to prosecute[183] may be entered at any time. Discovery was more likely to be under way. For other motion types, discovery was exceptional.

---

180. See appendix C.

181. Twenty-one cases listed in figure 8 as having been terminated by motion could not be classified by motion type and were excluded from figure 9.

182. Under rule 56(a), a claimant may move for summary judgment at any time after the expiration of 20 days from the commencement of the action; under rule 56(b), a defending party may so move at any time. In addition, under certain circumstances, a rule 12(b) motion may be treated as a rule 56 motion.

183. In the case sample, these rule 41(b) dismissals occurred for such reasons as failure of party to move for a default, nonattendance at a pretrial conference, and failure to pursue discovery.

FIGURE 8

PROPORTION OF DISCOVERED CASES FOR
TERMINATION CATEGORIES

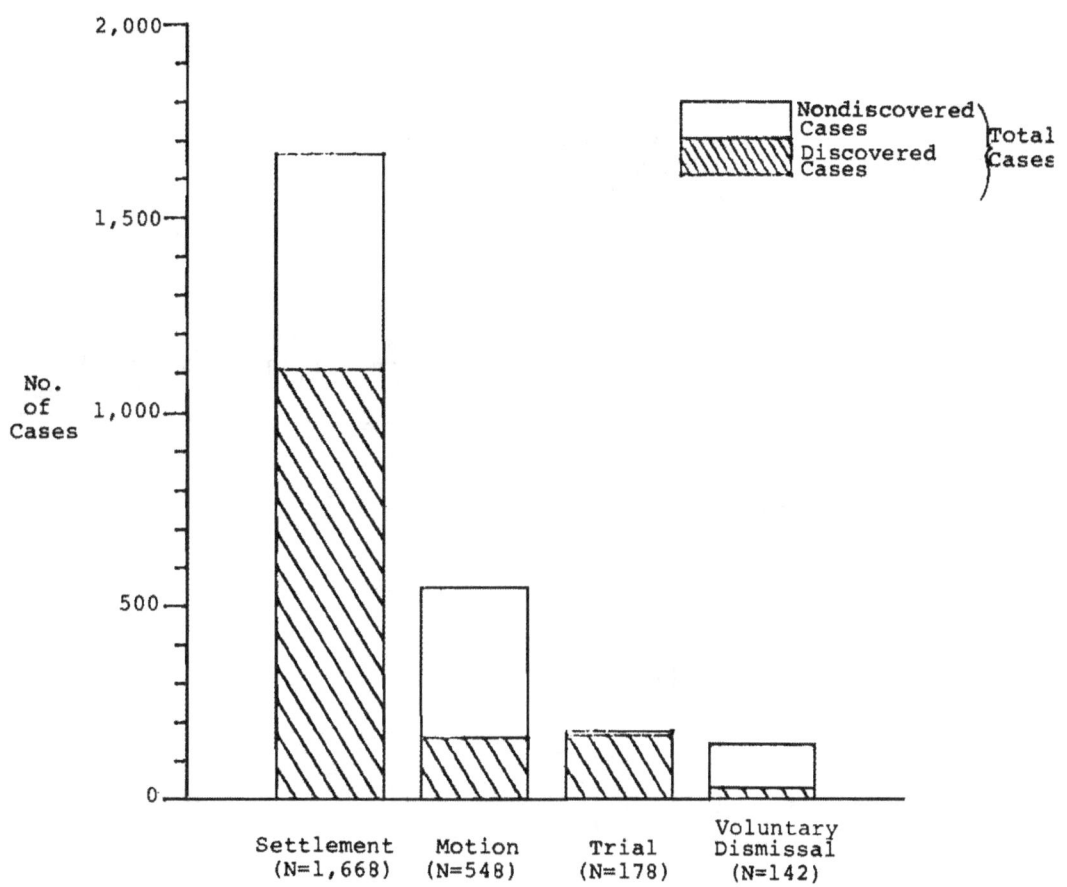

Note: Prisoner, administrative appeals, and seizure
cases were excluded.

FIGURE 9

PROPORTION OF DISCOVERED CASES
IN CASES TERMINATED BY MOTION,
BY MOTION TYPE

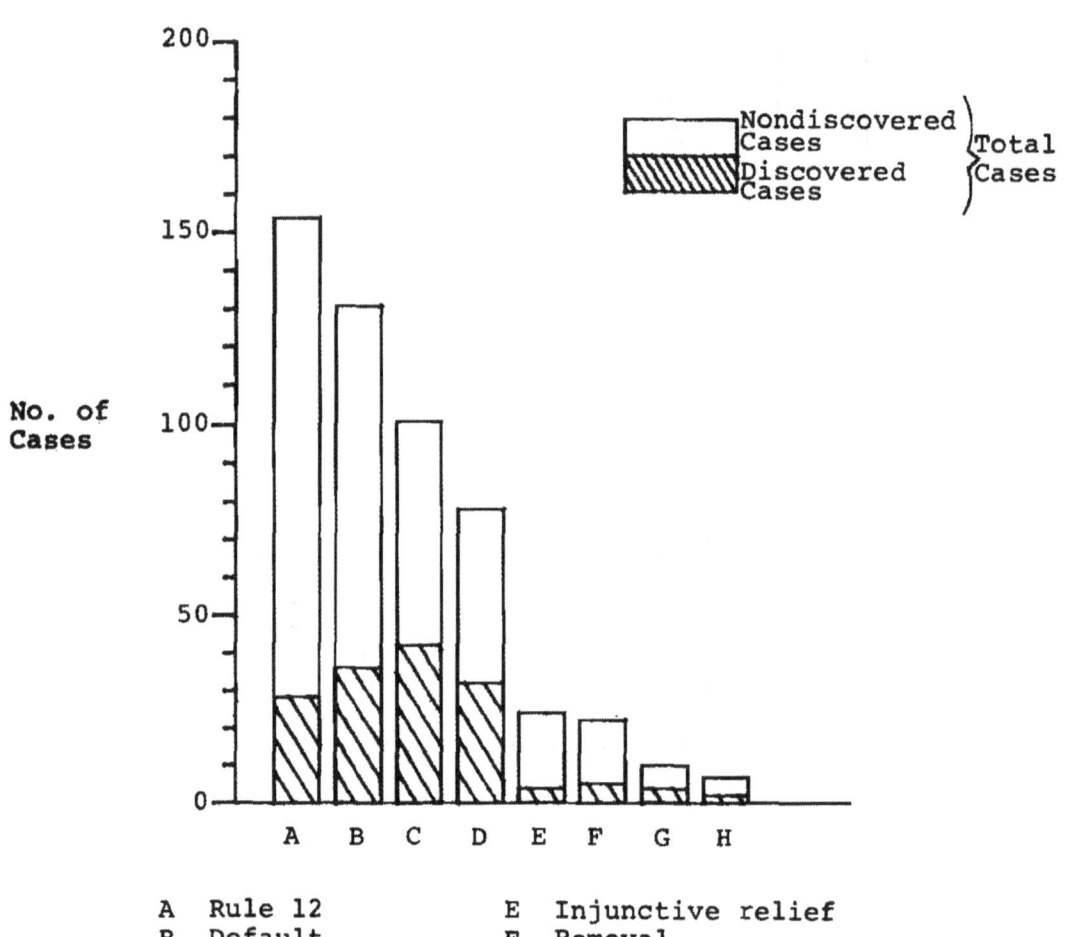

A  Rule 12              E  Injunctive relief
B  Default              F  Removal
C  Summary judgment     G  Other
D  Failure to           H  Transfer
   prosecute

Note:  Prisoner, administrative appeals, and
seizure cases were excluded.

✿ U.S. GOVERNMENT PRINTING OFFICE: 1986-161-392/50606

# THE FEDERAL JUDICIAL CENTER

The Federal Judicial Center is the research, development, and training arm of the federal judicial system. It was established by Congress in 1967 (28 U.S.C. §§ 620-629), on the recommendation of the Judicial Conference of the United States.

By statute, the Chief Justice of the United States is chairman of the Center's Board, which also includes the Director of the Administrative Office of the United States Courts and five judges elected by the Judicial Conference.

The Center's **Continuing Education and Training Division** conducts seminars, workshops, and short courses for all third-branch personnel. These programs range from orientation seminars for judges to on-site management training for supporting personnel.

The **Research Division** undertakes empirical and exploratory research on federal judicial processes, court management, and sentencing and its consequences, usually at the request of the Judicial Conference and its committees, the courts themselves, or other groups in the federal court system.

The **Innovations and Systems Development Division** designs and helps the courts implement new technologies, generally under the mantle of Courtran II—a multipurpose, computerized court and case management system developed by the division.

The **Inter-Judicial Affairs and Information Services Division** maintains liaison with state and foreign judges and judicial organizations. The Center's library, which specializes in judicial administration, is located within this division.

The Center's main facility is the historic Dolley Madison House, located on Lafayette Square in Washington, D.C.

Copies of Center publications can be obtained from the Center's Information Services office, 1520 H Street, N.W., Washington, D.C. 20005; the telephone number is 202/633-6365.